THE ISLAMIC TRILOGY
VOLUME 10

MOHAMMED, ALLAH,
AND POLITICS

THE ISLAMIC
POLITICAL DOCTRINE

THE ISLAMIC TRILOGY SERIES

THE ISLAMIC TRILOGY

VOLUME 10

MOHAMMED, ALLAH, AND POLITICS

THE ISLAMIC POLITICAL DOCTRINE

CENTER FOR THE STUDY
OF POLITICAL ISLAM

CSPI PUBLISHING

THE ISLAMIC TRILOGY
VOLUME 10

MOHAMMED, ALLAH, AND POLITICS

THE ISLAMIC POLITICAL DOCTRINE

COPYRIGHT © 2007
CSPI, LLC

ISBN 0-9785528-3-0
ISBN13 978-0-9785528-1

PUBLISHED BY CSPI, LLC
WWW.CSPIPUBLISHING.COM

PRINTED IN THE USA

TABLE OF CONTENTS

THE CSPI MAXIM

Islam is a political system, a culture, and a religion based upon the Koran, Sira, and Hadith. To understand Islam, know the Trilogy.

PURPOSE

The Center for the Study of Political Islam is dedicated to:
- *Making the political doctrine of the Koran, Sira, and Hadith (the Trilogy) available to the world.*
- *Establishing authoritative/verifiable fact-based knowledge.*
- *Integrating knowledge—using primary sources to give the complete picture of Islam's political doctrine.*

OVERVIEW

WHAT IS THIS BOOK?

This book is not about Islam; it is Islam. Islam has three sacred texts and this book is derived from these texts. Every paragraph can be verified in the source texts: the Koran, the Sira and the Hadith. Each chapter starts with a quote from the Koran reminding the reader that Mohammed's actions are to be followed in the smallest detail.

Islam is a religion, a culture, and the world's most successful political system. It is a fully developed political system and the oldest form of politics active today. Democracy has existed for just over 200 years, but political Islam is 1400 years old and is rapidly expanding its power and territory. In both the U.S. and Europe, Islamic political power is being felt. It is the goal of political Islam to replace all forms of government with Sharia law. Its doctrine is clearly spelled out in Islam's sacred texts. All of the doctrine that applies to the nonbeliever is found in this work.

RELIGIOUS AND POLITICAL ISLAM

The religion of Islam is what is required of a Muslim to enter Paradise and avoid Hell. Political Islam determines the treatment of unbelievers and the governance of Muslims. (The internal politics of Islam are not relevant here.)

The chief features of Islam, the religion, are:

Charity to other Muslims
Prayer to Allah
Fasting during the month of Ramadan
Pilgrimage to Mecca
Declaring that Mohammed is the prophet of the only god, Allah.

The majority of the Islamic texts are devoted to politics – how to treat the unbeliever. The religion of Islam is important to Muslims, but the politics affect everyone.

The foundation of Islam's legal and political system is clearly laid out in the Islamic Trilogy – the Koran, the Sira, and the Hadith. Every book of the Trilogy is both religious and political. More than half of the Koran focuses on the unbelievers. About three-quarters of the Sira (life of

Mohammed) is political. The Hadith is filled with political statements and examples. The fundamental principle of Islam is that its politics are sacred, perfect, eternal, and universal. All other political systems are man-made and must be replaced by Islamic law. Islam's success comes primarily from its politics.

In thirteen years as a spiritual leader, Mohammed converted 150 people to his religion. When he became a political leader and warrior, Islam exploded, and Mohammed became king of Arabia in ten years. He averaged a violent event every six weeks over the next nine years. These figures do not include assassinations and executions.

THE ISLAMIC TRILOGY

The political doctrine of Islam is found in the words of Allah (the Koran) and the words and actions of Mohammed (the Sunna). The Koran, is divided into two parts, the early part written in Mecca and the later part written in Medina. The Koran is filled with details of Mohammed's political and religious campaigns. Actual quotes of his political opponents, conversations, names, plots, insults, and threats are recorded. It is like reading a newspaper accounting, but it is not a biography. The Koran repeatedly states that Mohammed is the ideal pattern and his every word and action (*Sunna*) is an example of a sacred life. A Muslim always tries to imitate Mohammed in every way.

The words and actions of Mohammed are contained in two collections of texts—the Sira and the Hadith. His words and actions are considered to be Allah's divine pattern for all humanity.

The Sira is Mohammed's biography; the two most widely known versions are by Ibn Ishaq and Al Tabari. Approximately three-quarters of the Sira relates to politics and war.

A hadith, which means *tradition*, is a short story about what Mohammed did or said. A collection of hadiths is called a Hadith. There are many collections of hadiths, but the most authoritative are those by Bukhari and Abu Muslim.

So the Islamic Trilogy consists of:

> The Koran
> The Sira, or biographies, by Ishaq and Al Tabari
> The Hadith, or Traditions, by Bukhari and Muslim

The Trilogy is the foundation and totality of Islam. Every one of the hundreds of biographies of Mohammed is based upon the Sira and Hadith. Islam has a complete legal code, the Sharia, and all Islamic law is based upon the Trilogy. Every statement and action of political and religious Islam comes from the Trilogy. For example 9/11 was a political action based upon the Trilogy. If you know the Trilogy, you will see every news report about Islam with new eyes.

Islam believes that the Koran is the perfect, eternal, universal, final word of the only god, Allah. The Koran does not have the slightest error. It was brought to men by Mohammed who is the ideal pattern for all behavior of all peoples for all times, now and forever.

MAXIM

Islam is a political ideology. No action or statement by Islam can be understood without understanding its origins in the Trilogy. Any analysis, statement, or opinion about Islam is incomplete without a reference to the Trilogy. The Trilogy is the source and basis of all Islamic politics, diplomacy, history, philosophy, religion, and culture.

REFERENCE NUMBERS

The information in this book can be traced back to the source by use of the reference numbers:

I234 is a reference to Ibn Ishaq's *Sirat Rasul Allah*, translated by A. Guillaume as *The Life of Muhammad*. This is a reference to margin note 234.

T123 is a reference to *The History of al-Tabari* by the State University of New York. The number refers to the margin note 123.

M234 is a reference to *The Life of Mohammed* by Sir William Muir, AMS Press, New York, NY, 1975. The number is page 234.

B2,3,45 is a reference to Bukhari's Hadith. The three example numbers are volume 2, book 3, and number 45, a standard reference system.

M2,345 is a reference to Muslim's Hadith. The example would be book 2, number 345.

12:45 is Koran chapter (sura) 12, verse 45.

It is the present state of knowledge of the West about Islam that there is no standardized spelling of proper Arabic nouns. Examples: Muslim/Moslem, Mohammed/Muhammad.

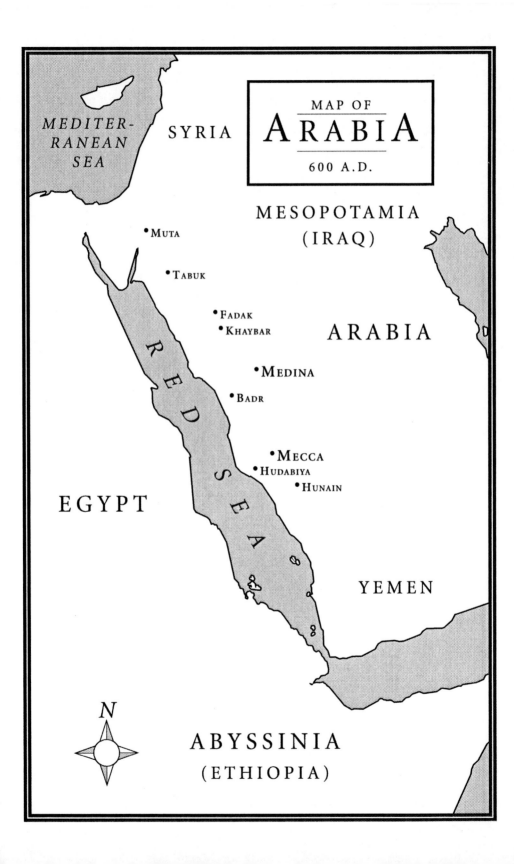

MEDITER-
RANEAN
SEA

SYRIA

MAP OF
ARABIA
600 A.D.

MESOPOTAMIA
(IRAQ)

•MUTA

•TABUK

•FADAK
•KHAYBAR

ARABIA

RED SEA

•MEDINA

•BADR

•MECCA
•HUDABIYA
•HUNAIN

EGYPT

YEMEN

N

ABYSSINIA
(ETHIOPIA)

IN THE BEGINNING

CHAPTER 1

33:21 You have an excellent example in Allah's Messenger
for those of you who put your hope in Allah and the
Last Day and who praise Allah continually.

· Read the preface, this is an unusual book.

Fourteen hundred years ago in Arabia, there was an orphan who became the first king of Arabia. Mohammed's name would become the most common name in the world. He was to create an empire that would dwarf the Roman Empire, and he was to become the ideal pattern for all men and make the god of the Arabs the god of all. The smallest aspect of his behavior would be recorded in great detail and would set the pattern of life for billions of people over the millennia.

Mohammed's father was called Abdullah, meaning slave of Allah. Allah was a high god of the many gods worshiped in the town of Mecca. His father died while his mother was pregnant. When he was five years old, his mother died and his grandfather took over his upbringing. Then Mohammed was orphaned for the third time when his grandfather died and his raising was assumed by his uncle, Abu Talib. All were of the Quraysh tribe. These brief facts are the history known about his early childhood.

CHILDHOOD

I115[1] When Mohammed was eight years old, his grandfather died. He was then taken in by Abu Talib, his uncle. His uncle took him on a trading trip to Syria, which was a very different place from Mecca. Syria was a sophisticated country that was Christian and very much a part of the cosmopolitan culture of the Mediterranean. It was Syrian Christians who gave the Arabs their alphabet. When Mohammed was a child there had never been a book written in Arabic, and only poems and business correspondence were written in Arabic.

---

1. The number is a reference to Ishaq's Sira Rasul Allah, the Sira.

MARRIAGE

1120 Mohammed was grown when he was hired by the wealthy widow and a distant cousin Khadija to act as her agent in trading with Syria. Mohammed had a reputation of good character and good business sense. Trading from Mecca to Syria was risky business because it took skill to manage a caravan and then to make the best deal in Syria. He managed Khadija's affairs well, and she returned a good profit on the trading.

1120 Khadija was a widow and well known among the Quraysh tribe. Sometime after hiring Mohammed as her business agent, she proposed marriage to him. They married and had six children. Their two sons died in childhood, and the four daughters lived to adulthood.

MONOTHEISM IN ARABIA

1144 After the destruction of Jerusalem by the Romans due to the Zealot's rebellion, Jews dispersed throughout the Middle East, so there was a strong presence of Jews in Arabia. There were a few Christians who were local Arabs, in fact, Mohammed's wife had a cousin who was a Christian. But the type of Christianity in the area of Mecca was unorthodox with a Trinity of God, Jesus and Mary.

1144 Jews and Christians were called the People of the Book. Since there was no book yet published in Arabic, this distinction was a strong one. The sources of the Arabic religions were found in oral tradition and custom. The Meccans were aware of the Jewish Abrahamic myths, and though Mecca was a long way from Syria where Abraham dwelt, the Meccans claimed that Abraham and Ishmael had built the Kabah in ancient times.

MECCA

BEGINNING TEACHINGS

CHAPTER 2

*4:13 These are the limits set up by Allah. Those who obey Allah
and His Messenger will be led into the Gardens watered by
flowing rivers to live forever. This is the ultimate reward!*

- All the world is divided into those who believe Mohammed and those who don't.
- When those who don't believe in Mohammed die, they will be tortured for eternity.
- Islam can use threats and beatings to settle arguments.
- Islam can single out, threaten, insult, and attack those who resist it.

At age 40 Mohammed had his first vision of whom he called the angel Gabriel. Mohammed told his revelations to his family and friends. Some joined with him in Islam (submission). His revelations began to mention the same Jewish stories found the Torah.

There would be a Day of Judgment and those who did not worship according to Mohammed's revelations would live in Hell. The Koran began to attack the native religions of Arabia as being false.

Mohammed's attacks on the religions of Mecca caused animosity. His opponents were promised torture for eternity. More arguments with Meccans followed. But many` Arabs were attracted to Islam as well.

I150 Mohammed would take month long retreats to be alone and do the Quraysh religious practices. After the retreat he would go and circumambulate (circle and pray) the Kabah.

I152 At the age of forty Mohammed began to have visions and hear voices. His visions were first shown to him as bright as daybreak during his sleep in the month of Ramadan. Mohammed said that the angel, Gabriel, came to him with a brocade with writing on it and commanded him to read. "What shall I read?" The angel pressed him and said, "Read."

Mohammed said again, "What shall I read?" The angel pressed him again tightly and again commanded, "Read!" Again the reply, "What shall I read?"

The angel said:

> 96:1 *Recite: In the name of your Lord, Who created man from clots of blood.*
> 96:3 *Recite: Your Lord is the most generous, Who taught the use of the pen and taught man what he did not know.*

T1150 Mohammed awoke from his sleep. Now Mohammed hated ecstatic poets and the insane. His thoughts were that he was now either a poet or insane, that which he hated. He thought to kill himself by jumping off a cliff. And off he went to do just that. Half way up the hill, he heard, "Mohammed, You are the apostle of Allah and I am Gabriel." He gazed at the angel and no matter which way he turned his head the vision followed his eyes. Mohammed stood there for a long time.

Then Mohammed began to receive what he called revelations such as:

> 74:1 *You [Mohammed], wrapped up in your robe, get up and sound the alarm.*
> 74:3 *Magnify your Lord. Purify your garment. Run from abomination. Do not give favors with the thought of reward. Wait patiently for your Lord. When the trumpet sounds, it will be a terrible day, a day without rest for the unbeliever.*
>
> 97:1 *Surely, We have revealed it [the Koran] on the night of power. And who will explain to you what the night of power is? The night of power is better than a thousand months. On that night the angels and the spirit descended with their Lord's permission, to do their every duty and all is peace until the break of day.*

THE FIRST CONVERT

I156 Mohammed's wife, Khadija, was the first convert. From the first she had encouraged him, believed him. She knew him to be of good character and did not think him to be deceived or crazy.

Soon he stopped hearing voices or seeing visions and became depressed and felt abandoned. Then his visions started again and said:

> 93:1 *By the brightness of the noonday sun and by the night at its darkest, your Lord has not forgotten you, and He does not hate you.*
> 93:4 *Certainly the future will be better than the past, and in the end your Lord will be generous to you, and you will be satisfied. Did He not find*

you living like an orphan and give you a home? Did He not find you lost and give you guidance? Did He not find you poor, and did He not give you enough?

Then Mohammed began to tell others who were close to him of words in his visions.

1:1 *In the Name of Allah, the Compassionate, the Merciful.*

1:2 *Praise be to Allah, Lord of the worlds. The Compassionate, the Merciful. King of the Judgment Day.*

1:5 *Only You do we worship, and to You alone do we ask for help. Keep us on the straight and narrow path. The path of those that You favor; not the path of those who anger You [the Jews] nor the path of those who go astray [the Christians].*

100:1 *By the snorting war steeds! And those whose hooves strike sparks of Fire! And those who press home the dawn attack! And raise clouds of dust, and slice through the enemy!*

100:6 *Truly, man is ungrateful to this Lord. He proves this with his actions. His love of wealth is passionate. Does he not know that when the graves are emptied and the secrets confined in men's hearts are revealed, that on that day their Lord will be perfectly informed about them?*

PRAYER

I157 Mohammed began to do his prayers with his new understanding. At first he did two prostrations with each prayer. Later he understood that he should use four prostrations per prayer and use two prostrations when he was traveling.

I158 Then when he was on a mountain he saw a vision in which Gabriel showed him how to do ritual ablutions as a purification ritual before prayer. He went home and showed his wife, Khadija, how he now understood the prayer rituals to be done and she copied him.

T1162 Mohammed, his wife and nephew, Ali, started praying at the Kabah with their new rituals of ablutions and prayer with prostrations. A visitor asked about this new ritual and was told that it was a new religion and that Mohammed said that he would receive the treasures of Rome and Persia.

THE FIRST MALES TO ACCEPT ISLAM

I159 A famine overtook the Quraysh and Mohammed's uncle Abu Talib had a large family. Abu Talib was a well respected tribal leader, but had fallen on hard times. Mohammed went to another uncle, Al Abbas, and they both went to Abu Talib and offered to help raise two of his children. Ali went into Mohammed's house to be raised by him and Khadija. When Ali turned ten he joined with Mohammed in his new religion, Islam.

1160 Mohammed and Ali used to go to the edge of town to practice their new ritual prayers. One day Abu Talib came upon them and asked what were they doing? Mohammed replied, "Uncle, this is the religion of Allah, His angels, His prophets and the religion of Abraham. Allah has sent me as an apostle to all mankind. You, my uncle, deserve that I should teach you the truth and call you to Islam." His uncle said that he could not give up the religion of his ancestors, but that he would support Mohammed.

The native Arabic religions were tribal in that every tribe had its deities, but the ceremonies and traditions were passed down by oral tradition, not in writing.

Mohammed lived in Mecca, which had been a religious center for many generations. It had a stone building that was roughly shaped like a cube and was called a Kabah. There were at least five other Kabahs in other towns in Arabia. The Kabah was a religious center for many of the native religions. Some sources say that there were as many as 360 deities worshipped in Mecca, a city that was profoundly polytheistic and tolerant. There were religious festivals that involved pilgrimages to Mecca, so at different times of the year, many tribes would gather to trade and do religious ceremonies.

One of the many gods in Mecca was Allah, a moon god. The native religions did not have any formal structure to the many deities, but Allah was a high god. Allah was the primary god of the Quraysh tribe of Mohammed, and Mohammed's father was named Abdullah, slave of Allah.

The idea of having an Arabian prophet was new. The sources of the native religions were unknown, but the new religion of Islam had a self-declared prophet. The Jews had prophets, and now the Arabs had a prophet in Mohammed.

Since Mohammed was a prophet, it was natural that the Koran should pick the thread of the history of the Jews and their prophets, such as Abraham and Moses.

Abraham:

> 51:24 *Have you heard the story of Abraham's honored guests? They went to him and said, "Peace!" And he replied, "Peace, strangers." And he went among his household and brought out a fatted calf, and he set it before them and said, "Do you want to eat?" They did not, and he became afraid of them. They said to him, "Do not be afraid," and gave him the news that*

> he was going to father a wise son. Abraham's wife came forward with a
> cry, striking her face, and said, "But I am old and barren!"
>
> 51:30 They said, "Your Lord says it is true, and he is wise and knowing."
>
> 51:31 Abraham said, "What errand are you on, messengers?" They replied,
> "We are sent to a wicked people, to shower them with stones of clay, sent
> by your Lord for their excesses."
>
> 51:35 We went to evacuate the believers in the city, but We only found
> one Muslim family, and We left signs warning those who fear the pain-
> ful punishment. Moses was another sign. We sent him to Pharaoh with
> manifest authority. But Pharaoh was confident of his might and turned
> his back and said, "You are a magician, or insane." So We seized him and
> his army and cast them into the sea, and he had only himself to blame.

Moses:

> 79: 15 Have you heard the story of Moses? How his Lord called to him in
> the sacred valley of Tuwa, saying, "Go to Pharaoh. He has rebelled, and
> say, 'Do you want to be purified?' Then I will guide you to your Lord so
> that you may fear Him."
>
> 79:20 And Moses showed Pharaoh a great miracle. But Pharaoh denied
> it and disobeyed. Furthermore, he turned his back and rebelled against
> Allah. He gathered an army and made a proclamation, saying, "I am
> your lord, the most high." So Allah punished him and made an example
> of him in this life and the hereafter. Surely this is a lesson for those who
> fear Allah.

Mohammed preached the doctrine of the Day of Judgment.

> 80:11 No, this [the Koran] is a warning! Let him who is willing, keep this in
> mind. It is written on honored pages, exalted and purified, by the hands
> of scribes, honorable and righteous.
>
> 80:16 Cursed be man! What has made him reject Allah? From what thing
> did Allah create him? He created him and molded him from a drop of
> sperm; then He made an easy path for him from the womb then caused
> him to die and put him in his grave. Then when He pleases, He will resur-
> rect him. But man has not yet fulfilled Allah's commands.
>
> 80:33 But when the trumpet blast sounds, a man will flee from his brother
> and his mother and his father and his wife and his children. That day,
> every man will be focused on his own concerns. There will be radiant
> faces that day, laughing and joyous, but other faces that day will have
> dust upon them and blackness will cover them. These are the unbelievers,
> the wicked.

After the Day of Doom would come Paradise for the believers and eternal
punishment for those who rejected Mohammed.

52:7 *Truly, a punishment from your Lord is coming, and no one can stop it. That day heaven will heave from side to side, and the mountains will shake to pieces. Woe on that day to those who called the messengers liars, who wasted their time in vain disputes.*

52:13 *On that day they will be thrown into the Fire of Hell. This is the Fire that you treated like a lie. What! Do you think that this is magic? Or, do you not see it? Burn there! Bear it patiently, or impatiently. It will all be the same to you, because you will certainly get what you deserve.*

52:17 *But those who have feared Allah will live pleasantly amid Gardens, rejoicing in what their Lord has given them, and what their Lord has protected them from, saying, "Eat and drink in health as a reward for your good deeds." They will recline on arranged couches, and We will marry them to dark-eyed houris [beautiful companions of pleasure].*

77:29 *They will be told, "Go to that Hell that you deny. Go to the shadows of smoke that rise in three columns, where there is no relief or shelter from the flame." The sparks flying out are like towers, yellow like tawny camels. Woe on that day to those who reject the truth!*

77:35 *They cannot speak that day, and they will not be allowed any excuses. Woe on that day to those who reject the truth!*

77:38 *This is the day of sorting, when We will collect you and your ancestors. If you have any tricks, try to trick Me. Woe on that day to those who reject the truth!*

56:27 *The people of the right-hand—Oh! How happy the people of the right-hand will be resting on raised couches amid thornless sidrahs [plum trees] and talh trees [banana trees], thick with fruit, and in extended shade and constantly flowing waters, and abundant fruits, neither forbidden nor out of reach. And We have specially made for them houris, companions, chaste and pure virgins, lovers and friends of equal age with them for the people of the right hand, a large number of the people of old, and a large number of the people of the latter generations.*

55:56 *There will be bashful virgins who gaze modestly, who have never been touched by either man nor jinn. Which of your Lord's blessings would you deny?*

55:58 *As lovely as rubies and pearls: which of your Lord's blessings would you deny?*

55:68 *In each, fruits and palms and pomegranates. Which of your Lord's blessings would you deny?*

55:70 *In each, fair and beautiful virgins. Which of your Lord's blessings would you deny?*

76:11 *But Allah saved them from the evil of that day and brought them happiness and joy. He rewarded their patience with Paradise and silk robes. Reclining on couches, none will suffer from extreme heat or cold.*

Trees will shade them, and fruit will dangle near by. Silver cups and crystal goblets will pass among them: silver cups, transparent as glass, their size reflecting the measure of one's deeds. They will be given ginger-flavored wine from the fountain called Salsabil. They will be waited on by eternally young boys. When you look at them you would think they were scattered pearls.

1161 There was added a new element to the religion. Any person who rejected the revelations of Mohammed would be eternally punished. The culture of religious tolerance in Mecca now had a new religion which preached the end of tolerance. Only Islam was acceptable.

1166 Since the word was out, Mohammed began to openly preach his new doctrine. He had been private for three years before he went public.

Mohammed spent a great deal of time arguing with the Meccans and telling them that they were doomed to Hell if they rejected him and his message. The Koran gives actual quotes of his doubters.

51:8 *You [Mohammed] are confused as what to say, but those who turn from the truth are turned aside by divine decree.*
51:10 *Cursed are the liars, who stumble along in the depths of ignorance! They ask, "When is the Judgment Day?" They will be tormented by the flames that day. "Have a taste of your torment, whose imminent arrival you denied."*
51:15 *But the Allah-fearing will live in Paradise amid gardens and fountains, enjoying what their Lord has given them, because they lived a good life. They slept little at night, and at dawn they prayed for forgiveness, and they gave a proper share of their wealth to the poor and outcast.*

69:44 *If he [Mohammed] had invented any of Our revelations, We would have grabbed him by the right hand, and cut his throat, and We would not have protected him from any of you.*
69:48 *But, surely, the Koran is a warning for the Allah-fearing. We know many think it is a lie. But it will cause grief for the unbelievers, because it is the absolute truth.*

1166 The Muslims went to the edge of Mecca to pray in order to be alone. One day a group of the Quraysh came upon them and began to mock them and a fight started. Sad, a Muslim, picked up the jaw bone of a camel and struck one of the Quraysh with it and bloodied him. This violence was the first blood to be shed in Islam.

1167 When Mohammed spoke about his new religion, it did not cause any problems among the Meccans. Then Mohammed began to condemn their religion and rituals and worship. This was a new phenomena. New religions could be added and had been, but not to the detriment to others.

The Meccans took offense and resolved to treat him as an enemy. Luckily, he had the protection of his influential uncle, Abu Talib.

1168 Some of the Quraysh went to Abu Talib, Mohammed's tribal protector, and said to him, "Your nephew has cursed our gods, insulted our religion, mocked our way of life, criticized our civilization, attacked our virtues, and said that our forefathers were ignorant and in error. You must stop him, or you must let us stop him. We will rid you of him." Abu Talib gave them a soft reply and sent them away.

1169 The Quraysh saw that Abu Talib would not help. Mohammed continued to preach Islam and attack them and their lives. Mecca was a small town, everybody knew everybody. Islam had split the town of Mecca and divided the ruling and priestly tribe. The Quraysh were attacked at the very ground of their social being.

1170 Things got much worse. Now there was open hostility in the town. Quarrels increased, arguments got very heated. Complete disharmony dominated the town. The tribe started to abuse the recently converted Muslims. But Mohammed's uncle Abu Talib was a respected elder and was able to protect them from real harm.

THE FAIR

Mecca was a town with two sources of money from the outside. The first was trading, and Mohammed had made his money in the caravan trade. The other was the fees from the pilgrims to the shrine of the Kabah. Fairs combined a little of both. All the tribes came for a fair. People would see old acquaintances and buy, sell or trade goods. Since Mecca was one of several sacred or pilgrim sites, rituals for the different tribal gods were performed around the Kabah and Mecca.

1171 It was time for the fair and the Quraysh were in turmoil. They were desperate that the divisions and rancor that had come with Mohammed's preaching not spread to the other clans outside Mecca. So a group of concerned Quraysh talked and decided to meet with Al Walid, a man of respect and influence. He told them that all the visitors would come to them and ask about this man Mohammed and what he was preaching. It was a foregone conclusion that Mohammed would preach and people would ask.

1171 But what could they agree on to tell the visitors so that there could be one voice. What would they call him? Was he possessed? Crazy? A ecstatic poet? A sorcerer? Who was he? What was he? Finally they agreed upon Mohammed being a sorcerer since he separated a son from his father or brother or wife or from his family.

68:1 *By the pen and by what the angels write, by the grace of your Lord, you [Mohammed] are not possessed! Certainly, a limitless reward awaits you, because you have a noble nature, but you will see and they will see, which of you is insane.*

53:1 *By the star when it sets, your companion [Mohammed] is not wrong, nor is he misled, and he does not speak out of his own desire.*

I171 So the Meccans split up and went out on the roadsides of town to speak with the travelers before they even arrived at Mecca.

I171 Mohammed delivered a message from Allah about the political leaders of the unbelievers. Indeed, many of the rich and powerful, who resisted Mohammed, earned their place in the Koran. The Koran gives such precise details and direct quotes of their arguments that if you were a Meccan of that day, you would know exactly who the person was.

96:6 *No, man is certainly stubborn. He sees himself as wealthy. Certainly, all things return to your Lord.*

96:9 *What do you think of a man [Abu Jahl] who holds back a servant of Allah [Mohammed] when he prays? Do you think that he is on the right path, or practices piety? Do you think that he treats the truth as a lie and turns his back? Does he not know that Allah sees everything?*

96:15 *No! Certainly if he does not stop, We will grab him by the forelock [cutting off or holding by the forelock was a shame in Arabic culture], the lying, sinful forelock! Let him call his comrades [the other Meccans]. We will call the guards of Hell. No, do not obey him, rather, adore and get closer to Allah.*

74:11 *Let Me deal with My creations, whom I have given great riches and sons to sit by their side, and whose lives I have made smooth and com- fortable. And still he [Al Walid] wants me to give him more. No, I say. He is an enemy of Our revelations. I will impose a dreadful punishment on him because he plotted and planned.*

74:19 *Damn him! How he planned. Again, Damn him! How he planned.*

74:21 *Then he looked around and frowned and scowled and turned his back with vain pride and said, "This is nothing but old magic; it is the work of a mere mortal."*

74:26 *We will certainly throw him into Hell.*

68:6 *Your Lord knows the man who strays from His path, and He knows who has been guided. Do not listen to those who treat you like a liar. They want you to compromise with them so that they may compromise with you.*

68:10 *Do not listen to the despicable person, who readily swears oaths, a defamer, going about with slander, enemy of the good, a transgressor, a criminal. He is cruel and impure from birth, though wealthy and blessed with sons. When Our wonderful verses are recited to him, he says "Fables of the ancients." We will brand him on the nose.*

111:1 *Let the hands of Abu Lahab [Mohammed's uncle and an opponent] die and let him die! His wealth and attainments will not help him. He will be burned in Hell, and his wife will carry the firewood, with a palm fiber rope around her neck.*

I172 The plan of hurting Mohammed by warning the visitors made everyone more curious. When they heard Mohammed's soaring words from the Koran many visitors were impressed. When they left they took all the stories from Mecca, the Quraysh, the new Muslims and then, of course, Mohammed. Soon all of that part of Arabia was talking.

I178 In what would be very fortuitous for Mohammed, the Arabs of Medina were attracted to Mohammed's message. Since half of their town were Jews, the Arabs of Medina were used to the talk of only one god.

PUBLIC TEACHING

CHAPTER 3

*3:32 Say: Obey Allah and His messenger, but if they reject it,
then truly, Allah does not love those who reject the faith.*

- The host culture (the native culture that Islam moves into) is attacked at all levels.
- Violence is promised to those who argue with Mohammed.
- Evil is defined as whatever resists Islam.
- All compromise between Islam and others is rejected. Islam is absolutely right.
- Those who resist Islam are singled out and verbally attacked.

As Mohammed continued to preach Islam, more arguments happened. More and more of the Koran is spent condemning those who disagree with Mohammed's words. The only true religion was Islam and all of the Meccans were wrong and enemies of Allah. Mohammed's opponents were doomed to Hell.

Local leaders tried to come to some compromise with Mohammed, but he asserted he was completely correct and the leaders were in absolute error. The community was torn up and divided.

The leaders tried to prove Mohammed wrong with arguments and demands for heavenly proof. Mohammed continued to argue that the Koran was the only proof of his divine mission that was needed.

All the other cultures that denied their prophets were destroyed by Allah. The Jewish stories now were given in the form that proved that everyone should listen to Mohammed.

The Koran continued in its insistence that Mohammed was the prophet of Allah. All the resistance to the words of Mohammed was evil. The Koran records the public campaign of Mohammed in Mecca.

At first Mohammed had only told close friends and relatives about his message. Now he began to move more into the public. The Koran condemns those who argue with Mohammed.

The Meccans reasoned that if the all knowing god of the universe was the author of the Koran, then why not deliver the entire Koran at once, instead of delivering it in piecemeal manner.

> 25:32 *Those who disbelieve say, "Why was the Koran not revealed to him all at once?" It was revealed one part at a time so that We might strengthen your heart with it and so that We might rehearse it with you gradually, in slow, well-arranged stages.*
>
> 25:33 *They will not come to you with any difficult questions for which We have not provided you the true and best answers. Those who will be gathered together face down in Hell will have the worst place and will be the farthest away from the right path.*

The arguments of those who disagree with Mohammed are false.

> 18:56 *We do not send messengers except as bearers of glad tidings and to give warnings. Yet the unbelievers make false contentions so that they may refute the truth. They mock Our signs just like they do Our warnings. Who is more unjust than he who is reminded of His Lord's signs but turns away from them and forgets what His hands have done? Truly We have placed veils over their hearts so that they do not understand, and deafness over their ears. Even if you give them guidance, they will not follow.*
>
> 21:92 *Truly, this religion of yours is the only religion, and I am your Lord, so worship Me. But they have broken their religion [Christianity] into sects, and yet they will all return to Us. Whoever does good things and believes will not have his efforts denied. We will record everything.*

I183 Mohammed continued to preach the glory of Allah and condemn the Quraysh religion. He told them their way of life was wrong, their ancestors would burn in Hell, he cursed their gods, he despised their religion and divided the community, setting one tribesman against the others. The Quraysh felt that this was all past bearing. Tolerance had always been their way. Many clans, many gods, many religions. Another religion was fine, why did Mohammed demean them?

> 21:16 *We did not create the heavens and the earth and everything in between for entertainment. If We had wanted a diversion, We could have found amusement in Our presence, as if We would ever do such a thing! No, We throw the truth at falsehood, and it crushes its head. There you have it: falsehood is destroyed! Woe to you for the lies you say about Us!*

1183 One day at the Kabah the Meccans were discussing Mohammed and his enmity towards them, when Mohammed arrived. He kissed the Black Stone of the Kabah and started past them as he circumambulated [walk around the Kabah and repeat prayers] the Kabah. Each time he passed by them they insulted him. On the third round, he stopped and said, "Listen to me, by Allah I will bring you slaughter." The Quraysh were stunned at his threat. They said, "Mohammed, you have never been a violent man, go away."

1184 The next day many of the Quraysh were at the Kabah when Mohammed arrived. They crowded around him and said, "Are you the one who condemned our gods and our religion?" Mohammed answered that he was the one. One of them grabbed him and Abu Bakr, Mohammed's chief follower, pressed forward and said, "Would you kill a man for saying that Allah is his Lord?" They let him go. This was worst treatment that Mohammed received in Mecca.

But Mohammed was not afraid. He was on a divine mission.

A TRIBAL CHIEF TRIES TO CUT A DEAL

1186 One day while the Quraysh were in council one of the chiefs, Utba, decided to approach Mohammed and see if he could make a deal that would please everybody. Things were only getting worse about Mohammed and the others said to go and try. So he went to the Kabah and there was Mohammed. "Nephew, you have come to us with an important matter. But you have divided the community, ridiculed our customs, and insulted our forefathers. See if any of my suggestions can help in this matter. If you want money, we will give you money. If you want honor we will make you our king. If you are possessed we will get you a physician."

1186 Mohammed said that he represented the only Allah. His teachings were beautiful, and then he began to recite the glorious poetry and imagery of the Koran. The tribal chief was impressed with the beauty of Mohammed's words and left.

1186 When the tribal chief returned to the Quraysh, he said, "Leave him alone, his words are beautiful. If other Arabs kill him, your problem is solved. If he becomes sovereign over all, you will share in his glory. His power will become your power and you can make money off his success." They replied that Mohammed had bewitched him.

Mecca was a small town and there were meetings about what to do about Mohammed.

86:15 *They plot and scheme against you [Mohammed], and I plot and scheme against them. Therefore, deal calmly with the unbelievers and leave them alone for a while.*

43:79 *Do they make plots against you? We also make plots. Do they think that We do not hear their secrets and their private conversations? We do, and Our messengers are there to record them.*

The Koran records some of the resistance of the Meccans to Mohammed.

38:1 *I swear by the Koran, full of warning! Truly, the unbelievers must be filled with arrogant pride to oppose you [Mohammed]. How many earlier generations did We destroy? In the end, they cried for mercy when there was no time to escape!*

38:4 *They are skeptical that a messenger would come to them from their own people, and the unbelievers say, "This man is a sorcerer and a liar! Has he combined all the gods into one Allah? That is an amazing thing!" And their chiefs [the leaders of the opposition to Mohammed in Mecca] went about and said, "Walk away. Remain faithful to your gods. This is a plot. We have never heard of such a thing in the earlier religion. This is nothing but an invented tale!"*

38:8 *They say, "Why, of all people, has the message been sent to him [Mohammed]?" Yes! They doubt My warnings because they have not tasted My vengeance. Do they possess the blessings of the mighty, your Lord's mercy? Is the kingdom of the heavens and the earth and everything in between in their hands? If so, let them climb up to the heavens if they can! Any allies [Mohammed's opponents] remaining here will be defeated.*

MORE ARGUMENTS WITH THE MECCANS

I188, 189 Another group of Meccans sent for Mohammed to see if they could negotiate away this painful division of the tribes. They went over old ground and again Mohammed refused the money and power that was offered. He said they were the ones who needed to decide whether they wanted to suffer in the next world and he had the only solution. If they rejected him and his message, Allah would tend to them. One of the Quraysh said, "Well, if you speak for and represent the only true god, then perhaps his Allah could do something for them."

"This land is dry. Let his Allah send them a river next to Mecca."

"They were cramped being next to the mountains. Let his Allah open up some space by moving the mountains back."

"Our best members are dead. Let your Allah renew them to life and in particular send back the best leader of our tribe, Qusayy. We will ask Qusayy whether or not you speak truly."

I189 Mohammed said that he was sent as a messenger, not to do such work. They could either accept his message or reject it and be subject to the loss. Then one of them said, "If you won't use your Allah to help us, then let your Allah help you. Send an angel to confirm you and prove to us that we are wrong. As long as the angel was present, let him make Mohammed a garden and fine home and present him with all the gold and silver he needed. If you do this, we will know that you represent Allah and we are wrong." The Quraysh wanted miracles as a proof.

> 25:7 *They say, "What kind of messenger is this? He eats food and walks the streets! Why has an angel not been sent down with him to assist in warning the people? Why has he not been given a great treasure or a rich garden to supply his needs?" The unjust say, "You are merely following a madman." See what kind of comparisons they make to you. They have gone astray and cannot find their way.*
>
> 25:20 *All of the messengers whom We sent before you were also men who ate food and walked the streets. We have made some of you a test for others. Will you be steadfast? Your Lord is watching everything.*
>
> 25:21 *Those who do not look forward to Our meeting say, "Why have angels not been sent down to us and why may we not see our Lord?" Obviously, they think too highly of themselves. Their impiety is insolent and scornful!*

> 15:4 *We never destroy a city whose term was not preordained. No nation can delay or change its destiny. They say: "You [Mohammed] to whom the message was revealed, you are surely insane. If you were telling the truth, why did you not bring angels to us?"*
>
> 15:8 *We do not send the angels without good reason. If We did, the unbelievers would still not understand. Surely, We have sent down the message, and surely, We will guard it. Before your time, We sent apostles to the sects of the ancient peoples, but they mocked every messenger. Similarly, We allow doubt to enter the hearts of the sinners. They do not believe it, even though the example of the ancients has preceded them. Even if We opened a gate into heaven for them the entire time they ascended, they would say, "Our eyes are playing tricks on us. No, we are bewitched."*

I189 Mohammed did not do miracles, because such things were not what Allah had appointed him to do.

I189 Then one of the Quraysh said, "Then let the heavens be dropped on us in pieces as you say your Lord could do. Then if you do not we will not believe." Mohammed said that Allah could do that if Allah wished or he might not if he wished.

I189 They then said, "Did not your Lord know that we would ask you these questions? Then your Lord could have prepared you with better answers. And your Lord could have told you what to tell us if we don't believe. We hear that you are getting this Koran from a man named Al Rahman from another town. We don't believe in Al Rahman. Our conscience is clear. We must either destroy you or you must destroy us. Bring your angels and we will believe them."

1190 Mohammed turned and left. A cousin chased him and fell in beside him to talk. He said, "Mohammed, your tribe has made you propositions and you have rejected them. First, they asked you for things for themselves that they might see if you are true. Then they would follow you. You did nothing. Then they asked you for things for yourself so they could see your superiority over them and prove your standing with Allah. You did nothing. Then they said to bring on the punishments that your Allah has told you about and you have frightened us with his threats. You did nothing. Personally, I will never believe until you get a ladder up to the sky, you will climb it while I watch, and four angels will come and testify that you are truthful. But you know, even if you did all that, I still don't know if I would believe you."

1190 Mohammed went home and was sad and depressed. He had hoped when they sent for him it was to announce their submission to his Allah and his teachings. Instead, it was resistance and questions.

1191 Mohammed would come to the Kabah and tell the Meccans what terrible punishments that Allah had delivered to the others in history who had not believed their prophets. That was now one of his constant themes. Allah punished others like you who did not listen to men like me.

> 44:9 *They [the Meccans] fool around in doubt, but watch them the day the sky emits a visible smoke that will cover mankind. This will be a terrible punishment. They will cry, "Lord, take away our punishment. We are believers." But how did warning them help when Our messenger went to them, and they rejected him and said, "He learned it from others, he is insane!"? If We were to give you any respite, you would surely revert to wickedness. On the day when We seize you with a terrible onslaught, We will certainly inflict punishment!*

1191 One of the Quraysh, Al Nadr, had been to Persia and had learned many tales and sagas from the story tellers there. The traveler would announce, "I can tell a better tale than Mohammed." Then he would proceed to tell them ancient sagas and stories of Persia. "In what way is Mohammed a better story teller than me?"

1192 Since Mohammed and the Koran claimed Jewish roots, the Quraysh decided to send their story teller to the Jews in Medina and ask for help. This was not a causal quest, as it took the better part of a month for the trip and questions. So Al Nadr went to Medina and asked the rabbis what questions to ask Mohammed. He told the rabbis about Mohammed, what he did, what he said and that he claimed to be a prophet. Since they had had prophets they must know more about the subject than the Meccans.

1192 The rabbis said, "Ask him these three questions. If he knows the answer then he is a prophet, if not then he is a fake."

"What happened to the young men who disappeared in ancient days."

"Ask him about the mighty traveler who reached the ends of the East and the West."

"Ask him, What is the spirit?"

1192 Back in Mecca, they went to Mohammed and asked him the three questions. He said he would get back to them tomorrow. Days went by. Finally, fifteen days had passed. Mohammed waited on Gabriel for the answers. The Meccans began to talk. Mohammed did not know what to do. He had no answers. Finally, he had a vision of Gabriel.

The Koran answered all the questions and statements of the Quraysh. As to the question about the mighty traveler:

> 18:83 *They will ask you about Zul-Qarnain [Alexander, the Great]. Say: I will recite to you an account of him. We established his power in the land and gave him the means to achieve any of his aims. So he followed a path, until, when he reached the setting of the sun, he found it setting in a muddy pond. Near by he found a people. We said, "Zul-Qarnain, you have the authority to either punish them or to show them kindness."*
>
> 18:87 *He said, "Whoever does wrong, we will certainly punish. Then he will be returned to his Lord, Who will punish him with a terrible punishment. But whoever believes and does good deeds shall be given a wonderful reward, and We will give them easy commands to obey."*
>
> 18:89 *Then he followed another path, until, when he came to the rising of the sun, he found that it rose upon a people to whom We had given no protection from it. He left them as they were. We knew everything about him. Then he followed another path until, when he reached a place between two mountains, he found a people living in a valley who could scarcely understand a single word. They said, "Zul-Qarnain, the people of Gog and Magog are terrorizing the land. May we pay you tribute so that you will build a strong barrier between us and them?"*
>
> 18:95 *He said, "The power which my Lord has given me is better than your tribute. Help me, therefore, with manpower. I will build a strong barrier between you and them. Bring me blocks of iron." Later, when he had filled the gap between the two mountains, he said, "Blow with your bellows!" When it had become as red as fire, he said, "Bring me molten lead to pour over it." So the people of Gog and Magog were unable to climb over the barrier or to go through it. He said, "This is a mercy from*

my Lord, but when my Lord's promise comes to pass, He will destroy it, because my Lord's promises always come true."

The Quraysh had questions about proof of Mohammed's messages. Here is the Koran's restatement of their questions about angels coming, creating rivers, creating wealth and any other miracle to prove Mohammed's validity. The Koran's response:

17:88 *Say: If men and jinn were assembled to produce something like this Koran, they could not produce its equal, even though they assisted each other. And certainly in this Koran We have explained to man every kind of argument, and yet most men refuse everything except disbelief. They [the Meccans] say, "We will not believe in you until you cause a spring to gush forth from the earth for us; or until you have a garden of date trees and grape vines, and cause rivers to gush abundantly in their midst; or when you cause the sky to fall down in pieces, as you claim will happen; or when you bring us face-to-face with Allah and the angels; or when you have a house of gold; or when you ascend into heaven; and even then we will not believe in your ascension until you bring down a book for us which we may read." Say: Glory be to my Lord! Am I nothing except a man, a messenger?*

17:94 *What keeps men from believing when guidance has come to them but that they say, "Has Allah sent a man like us to be His messenger?" Say: If angels walked the earth, We would have sent down from heaven an angel as Our messenger. Say: Allah is a sufficient witness between you and me. He is well acquainted with His servants and He sees everything.* 17:97 *Whoever Allah guides, he is a follower of the right way, and whoever He causes to err, they shall not find any to assist them but Him. We will gather them together on the Resurrection Day, face down, blind, deaf, and dumb. Hell will be their home. Every time its flames die down, We will add fuel to the Fire. This is their reward because they did not believe Our signs and said, "When we are reduced to bones and dust, will we really be raised up as a new creation?"*

As regards to the old Persian stories that are as good as Mohammed's:

25:3 *Still they have worshiped other gods, besides Him, who have created nothing and were themselves created. They are powerless to work good or evil for themselves, nor can they control life or death or resurrection. But the unbelievers say, "This [the Koran] is nothing but a lie which he [Mohammed] has created with the assistance of others producing slander and injustice."* 25:5 *They say, " These are ancient fables that he has written down. They are dictated to him morning and night."*

25:6 Say: The Koran was revealed by Him who knows the secrets of the heavens and the earth. He is truly forgiving and merciful.

As for following the religion of their forefathers:

43:21 Are they clinging to a scripture that We had given them earlier? No! They say, "Our fathers followed a certain religion, and we are guided by their footsteps." And so, whenever We sent a messenger before you to an erring people, their wealthy said, "Our fathers followed a certain religion, and we are guided by their footsteps." The messenger said, "What! Even if I bring you better guidance than your fathers had?" They replied, "We do not believe what you say." So We punished them. Now see what comes to those who reject truth!

THE QURAYSH LISTEN TO MOHAMMED'S READING

1203 Three of the Meccans decided, each on their own, to sit outside Mohammed's house and listen to him recite the Koran and pray. As they left they ran into each other. They said that they should not do it again as someone might think that they cause others to listen. But on the next night they all three did the same thing. And so on the third night as well. They then talked among each other. One said, "I heard things I know and know what was meant by them. And I heard things I don't know and I don't know what was intended by them." The other agreed. The third said that he had always had a competition with one of Mohammed's recent converts. They had both fed the poor and helped the oppressed. They had always been as equals, but now his friendly rival claimed that he had a prophet and his friend did not. Hence, he was now superior. He said, "But I can never believe in this man, Mohammed."

1204 So the next time Mohammed called upon them to submit to Islam, they said, "Our hearts are veiled; we don't understand what you say. There is something in our ears so we can't hear you. A curtain divides us. You go follow your path and we will go ours."

The Koranic response:

17:45 When you recite the Koran, We place an invisible barrier between you and the unbelievers. We place veils over their hearts and deafness in their ears so that they do not understand it, and when you mention only your Lord, Allah, in the Koran, they turn their backs and flee from the truth. We know absolutely what they listen to when they listen to you, and when they speak privately, the wicked say, "You follow a mad man!" See what they compare you to. But they have gone astray and cannot find the way.

22

17:49 *They say, "When we are nothing but bones and dust, will we really be raised up from the dead to be a new creation?" Say: Yes, whether you be stones, or iron, or any other thing which you conceive to be harder to resurrect." When they say, "Who will bring us back to life?" Say: He who created you the first time. They will shake their heads at you and say, "When will this happen?" Say to them, "Perhaps it will be soon—a day when He will call you, and you will answer by praising Him, and you will think that you have waited only a little while!"*

Mohammed's opponents are frequently quoted and paraphrased:

43:29 *I have allowed these men and their fathers to enjoy the pleasurable things of this life until the truth comes to them and a messenger makes things clear.*
43:30 *But when the truth came to them, they said: "This is trickery, and we reject it." And they say, "Why was this Koran not revealed to a great man of one of the two cities [Mecca and Taif]?"*
43:32 *Will they distribute Allah's mercy? We distribute among them their worldly success, and We exalt some of them above the others in ranks, subjecting some to others. Your Lord's mercy is greater than the wealth they amass. And if it were not probable that all humanity might become a single nation of unbelievers, We would have given silver roofs and staircases to everyone, and silver doors for their homes, and silver couches on which to recline, and ornaments of gold, but these are merely luxuries of this world's life. The afterlife with your Lord is for the righteous.*
43:36 *We assign a devil as a companion for those who turn their backs and neglect to remember Allah. Satan will certainly turn man from the way of Allah, even though he believes he is being guided correctly. On the day when man comes before Us, he will say, "Satan, I wish that the distance between east and west separated us." Satan is a wretched companion. But that realization will not help you that day, because you were unjust, and you will share the punishment. Can you make the deaf listen or guide the blind and those clearly in error?*

21:5 *They say, "No, This is nothing but jumbled dreams. He made it up. He is just a crazy poet! We want him to bring us a sign similar to those given to the prophets of the past!" Up to their time, despite Our warnings, not a single city that We destroyed believed. Will these people believe?*
21:7 *Before you, Our messengers were also men to whom We sent a revelation. If you do not know this, you should ask someone who has received the Message. We did not give them bodies that did not need food, and they would not live forever. In the end, We kept Our promise, and We saved whom We pleased and destroyed the sinners. Now We have given you a book [the Koran] that contains the message for you. Now will you understand?*

21:11 *How many wicked cities have We destroyed and replaced with another people? And still, when they sensed Our punishment, they began to run. It was said to them, "Do not run. Return to your homes and easy lives so that you may be called to account for your actions." They said, "Oh no! We were certainly wicked!" This cry of theirs did not stop until We mowed them down and left them like reaped corn.*

And then there are arguments that give the Koranic view of Christianity:

43:81 *Say to the Christians: If Allah, the most gracious, had a son, I would be the first to worship. Glory to the Lord of the heavens and the earth, the Lord of the throne! He is free from the things attributed to Him! So leave them to chatter on and play with words until they meet the day they are promised.*

43:84 *Allah rules the heavens and the earth. He is the wise, the knowing. Blessed is He whose kingdom is the heavens and the earth and everything in between. He has knowledge of the Hour of Judgment, and you will be returned to Him.*

43:86 *Those whom they invoke for protection besides Allah have no power to intercede. Only He who bears witness to the truth may do that, and they know Him. If you asked them who their creator is, they would certainly say, "Allah." Then, how are they turned from the truth? And the Prophet will cry, "My Lord, truly these are people who do not believe." So turn away from them and say, "Peace." They will soon find out.*

Allah controls all things, including people who reject Islam.

6:25 *Some among them listen to you [Mohammed], but We have cast veils over their hearts and a heaviness to their ears so that they cannot understand our signs [the Koran]. If they see every sign, they will not have faith in them, but when they come to you, they will dispute with you, and the unbelievers will say, "This is only the fables of the old ones."*

2:6 *As for the unbelievers, whether you warn them or not, they will not believe. Their hearts and ears are sealed up by Allah, and their eyes are covered as well. There will be a dreadful doom awaiting them.*

7:179 *We have created many of the jinn and men for Hell. They have hearts with which they cannot understand, eyes with which they cannot see, and ears with which they cannot hear. They are like cattle—no, even worse, for they are neglectful.*

STRUGGLES

CHAPTER 4

8:20 Believers! Be obedient to Allah and His messenger, and
do not turn your backs now that you know the truth. Do
not be like the ones who say, "We hear," but do not obey.

- When the host culture tries to resist Islam, Islam is relentless and never tires of the attack.
- A Muslim is not a friend to a non-Muslim, not even family.

The Meccans began to resist Mohammed. A story teller said he could tell better stories. The Koran condemned him. Again and again the Koran condemned all those who resisted Islam to eternal torture in Hell.

The Meccans demanded proof that Mohammed was not just making up his revelations. Other leaders tried to strike a compromise to return to the old peace before Islam.

More arguments went back and forth, with the Koran continuing to assert Mohammed's mission and asserting that all who disagreed with Mohammed would go to Hell.

More Meccans began to believe Mohammed. There was a larger gulf between Muslims and their old friends.

Mohammed had one of his most famous visions, the night journey to Paradise. Mohammed was shown to be the final and ultimate prophet of Allah.

The Meccans demanded miracles to prove Mohammed's mission, but their demands for proof condemned them to Hell.

Mohammed's uncle had always protected him from the Meccans and now his uncle died as a non-Muslim. Then Mohammed's wife died. Mohammed soon had a new bride.

1217 Each of the clans of the Quraysh began to persecute those Muslims that they had any power over. If Mohammed attacked them, they would attack him through his converts. One slave, Bilal (to become famous later) was physically abused by being placed in the hot sun with a huge rock on his chest and being told to deny Islam. He refused. This was repeated until Abu Bakr, a chief Muslim, took notice and asked how long the owner would abuse him. The owner said, "You are one of those who corrupted him, you save him." So Abu Bakr offered to trade a stronger black, non-Muslim slave for Bilal. Then Abu Bakr freed Bilal. Abu Bakr did this with six other Muslim slaves as well.

I235 A Meccan met Mohammed and said, "Mohammed, you stop cursing our gods or we will start cursing your Allah." So Mohammed stopped cursing the Meccan gods. An ongoing theme of Mohammed's was of ancient civilizations who did not listen to their prophets and the terrible downfall of that country.

> 7:73 *And to Thamud's people [Thamud lay on an old trade route, north of Mecca. It was abandoned in Mohammed's day] We sent their brother Salih. He said, "Oh, my people! Worship Allah. You have no other god than Him, and clear proof has come to you from the Lord. This she-camel of Allah is a sign to you, so let her graze on Allah's earth and do not harm her, or you will be seized with a grievous punishment.*
>
> 7:74 *"Remember how He made you inheritors to the Adites and settled you in the land so that you build castles on the plains and build houses into the hills? So remember the benefits of Allah, and refrain from evil and corruption on the earth."*
>
> 7:75 *The chiefs of his people, who were scornful, said to those whom they thought were weak, even to those of them who believed, "Do you know for certain that Salih is sent by his Lord?" They said, "We do believe in the signs that have been sent through him."*
>
> 7:76 *Those who were scornful said, "We reject the signs in which you believe."*
>
> 7:77 *So they killed the she-camel and revolted against their Lord's command and said, "Oh, Salih, bring about your threats if you are a messenger sent by Allah." Then the earthquake seized them, and in the morning they were found dead on their faces in their homes.*
>
> 7:79 *So he turned away from them and said, "Oh, my people! I delivered my Lord's message to you, and I gave you good advice, but you do not love good advice."*

I235 A story teller boasted that he could tell better old stories and would tell them in competition with Mohammed. But the story teller was an unbeliever and the Koran condemned him, as well as all unbelievers.

> 31:6 *There are men who engage in idle tales [A Persian story-teller in Mecca said that his stories were better than Mohammed's] without knowing,*

and they mislead others from the way of Allah and turn it to scorn. There will be a shameful punishment for them. When Our signs are revealed to him, he turns away in arrogance as if he had not heard them, as though there were deafness in his ears. Give him tidings of a terrible punishment. Those who will believe and do good works, will enjoy the Gardens of Bliss, where they will abide forever. It is Allah's true promise, and He is mighty and wise.

1238 A Meccan took an old bone to Mohammed, crumbled it up and blew the dust towards Mohammed. He asked, "Will your Allah revive this bone?" Mohammed said, "Yes, I do say that. Allah will resurrect this bone and you will die. Then Allah will send you to Hell!"

1239 Some Meccans approached Mohammed and said, "Let us worship what you worship. Then you worship what we worship. If what you worship is better than what we worship, then we will take a share of your worship. And if what we worship is better, then you can take a share of that." The Koran's reply:

10:105 *And set your face toward the true religion, sound in faith, and do not be of those who revere other gods besides Allah. Do not call on gods besides Allah who cannot help or hurt you. If you do this, you will be one of the wrongdoers. And if Allah afflicts you with harm, there is no one who can remove it but Him, and if He intends good for you, no one can hold it back. He strikes whichever servant He pleases, and He is the gracious and the merciful.*

Islam means submission and that is what all must do. The only religion in Allah's eyes is Islam.

39:32 *Who does more wrong than one who lies against Allah and rejects the truth when it comes to him as a lie? Is there not a home in Hell for the blasphemers? The dutiful bring the truth and believe it to be the truth. They will have whatever they desire from their Lord. This is the reward of the good. Allah will disregard the worst of what they did and reward them for the best they did.*

39:36 *Is Allah not sufficient for His servant? They try to scare you with other gods besides Him, but there is no guide for him whom Allah sends astray. Whomever Allah guides, no one can lead astray. Is not Allah, almighty, able to enforce His will?*

THE SATANIC VERSES

T11921 Mohammed was always thinking of how he could persuade all the Meccans. It came to him that the three gods of the Quraysh could

1.   The T references are to Al Tabari's *History of Prophets and Kings.*

intercede with Allah. Mohammed said, "These are the exalted high flying cranes whose intercession is approved." The Meccans were delighted and happy. When Mohammed lead prayers at the Kabah, all the Meccans, Muslim and non-Muslim, took part. The Quraysh hung about after the combined service and remarked how happy they were. The tribe had been unified in worship, as before Islam.

T1192 When the news reached Ethiopia, some of the Muslims started for home. But then, trouble. The Koran revealed that Mohammed was wrong. Meccan gods could have no part in his religion. Satan had made him say those terrible words about how the other gods could help Allah. The retraction by Mohammed made the relations between Islam and the Meccans far worse than it had ever been.

THE POET'S SUBMISSION

I252 Al Dausi was a poet of some standing in Arabia and when he visited Mecca he was warned to stay away from Mohammed. Mohammed had hurt the Quraysh and broken the harmony of the tribe. He was warned that Mohammed could bring such divisions to his own family. But Al Dausi went to the mosque and there was Mohammed. Since he had been warned about Mohammed this made Al Dausi more curious to hear what Mohammed said when he prayed. He liked what he heard and followed Mohammed home. They spoke for some time and Al Dausi decided to submit to Islam.

I253 He returned home. His father was old and came to greet his son. Al Dausi said to him, "Go away father, for I want nothing to do with you or you with me." His father said, "Why, my son?" Al Dausi said, "I have become a Muslim." The father replied, "Well, then I shall do so as well."

I253 He then entered his home and told his wife, "Leave me, I want nothing to do with you." She cried, "Why?" Al Dausi said, "Islam has divided us and I now follow Mohammed." She replied, "Then your religion is my religion." He then instructed her in Islam.

The Koran is constant in its admonitions about whom a Muslim should be friends with.

> 3:28 *Believers should not take unbelievers as friends in preference to other believers. Those who do this will have none of Allah's protection and will only have themselves as guards. Allah warns you to fear Him for all will return to Him.*

> 9:23 *Oh, Believers, do not make friends of your fathers or your brothers if they love unbelief above Islam. He who makes them his friends does wrong. Say: If your fathers, and your sons, and your brothers, and your*

wives, and your kin-folks, and the wealth which you have gained, and the merchandise that you fear you will not sell, and the dwellings in which you delight—if all are dearer to you than Allah and His Messenger and efforts on His Path, then wait until Allah's command comes to pass. Allah does not guide the impious.

3:118 *Believers! Do not become friends with anyone except your own people. The unbelievers will not rest until they have corrupted you. They wish nothing but your ruin. Their hatred of you is made clear by their words, but even greater hatred is hidden within their hearts. We have made Our signs clear to you. Therefore, do your best to comprehend them.*

4:138 *Warn the hypocrites that torturous punishment awaits them. The hypocrites take unbelievers as friends rather than believers. Do they look for honor at their hands? Truly all honor belongs to Allah.*

4:144 *Believers! Do not take unbelievers as friends over fellow believers. Would you give Allah a clear reason to punish you?*

60:1 *Oh, you who believe, do not take My enemy and yours for friends by showing them kindness. They reject the truth that has come to you. They drive out the messengers and yourselves because you believe in Allah, your Lord. If you continue to fight for Allah's cause [jihad] and from a desire to please Me, would you show them kindness in private? I know best what you conceal and what you reveal. Whoever does this among you has already strayed from the right path.*

60:13 *Oh, Believers, do not enter into friendship with those against whom Allah is angered. They have despaired of the hereafter, even as the unbelievers despair of those who are in graves.*

5:57 *Oh, you who believe, do not take those who have received the Scriptures [Jews and Christians] before you, who have scoffed and jested at your religion, or who are unbelievers for your friends. Fear Allah if you are true believers. When you call to prayer, they make it a mockery and a joke. This is because they are a people who do not understand.*

I260 There was one Christian in Mecca in whom Mohammed took an interest. In the market there was a Christian slave who ran a booth. Mohammed would go and speak with him at length. This led to the Quraysh saying that what Mohammed said in the Koran, came from the Christian slave.

16:102 *Say: The Holy Spirit [Gabriel] has truthfully revealed it from your Lord so that it may confirm the faith of those who believe and be a guide and good news for those who submit. We know that they say, "It is a man that teaches him." The man [his name is uncertain] they point to speaks a foreign language while this is clear Arabic.*

29

THE NIGHT JOURNEY

1264 One night as he lay sleeping, Mohammed said that the angel nudged him with his foot. He awoke, saw nothing, and went back to sleep. This happened again. Then it happened a third time. Mohammed awoke, saw Gabriel and took his arm. They went out the door and found a white animal, half mule and half donkey. Its feet had wings and could move to the horizon at one step. Gabriel put Mohammed on the white animal and off they went to Jerusalem to the site of the Temple.

1264 There at the temple were Jesus, Abraham, Moses, and other prophets. Mohammed led them in prayer. Gabriel brought Mohammed two bowls. One was filled with wine and the other was filled with milk. Mohammed took the one with milk and drank it. That was the right choice.

1265 When Mohammed told this story at the Kabah, the Quraysh hooted at the absurdity of it. Actually, some of the Muslims found it too hard to believe and left Islam. One of them went to Abu Bakr and told him that Mohammed had gone to Jerusalem the night before. Bakr said they were lying. They told him to go and hear for himself. Mohammed was at the mosque telling of his story. Abu Bakr said, "If he says it, then it is true. He tells me of communication with Allah that comes to him at all hours of the day and night. I believe him."

1265 Aisha, Mohammed's favorite wife, said that Mohammed never left the bed that night, however, his spirit soared.

1266 Mohammed reported that Abraham looked exactly like him. Moses was a ruddy faced man, tall, thin, and with curly hair. Jesus was light skinned with reddish complexion and freckles and lank hair.

1268 After the prayers had been done in Jerusalem, Gabriel brought a fine ladder. Mohammed and Gabriel climbed the ladder until they came to one of the gates of heaven, called Gate of the Watchers. An angel was in charge there and had under his command 12,000 angels. And each of those 12,000 angels had 12,000 angels under them. The guardian angel asked Gabriel who Mohammed was. When Gabriel said it was Mohammed, the angel wished Mohammed well.

1268 All the angels who greeted Mohammed, smiled and wished him well, except for one. Mohammed asked Gabriel who was the unsmiling angel. The unsmiling angel was Malik, the Keeper of Hell. Mohammed asked Gabriel to ask Malik if he would show him Hell. So Malik removed the lid to Hell and flames blazed into the air. Mohammed quickly ask for the lid to be put back on Hell.

1269 At the lowest heaven, a man sat with the spirits of men passing in front of him. To one he would say, "A good spirit from a good body." And to another spirit he would say, "An evil spirit from an evil body." Mohammed asked who the man was. It was Adam reviewing the spirits of his children. The spirit of a believer excited him and the spirit of an infidel disgusted him.

1270 Then Mohammed was taken up to the second heaven and saw Jesus and his cousin, John, son of Zakariah. In the third heaven he saw Joseph, son of Jacob. In the fourth heaven, Mohammed saw Idris. In the fifth heaven was a man with a long beard and white hair. He was a very handsome man who was Aaron, son of Imran. In the sixth heaven was a dark man with a hooked nose. This was Moses. In the seventh heaven was a man sitting on a throne in front of a mansion. Every day 70,000 angels went into the mansion, not to come out until the day of resurrection. The man on the throne looked just like Mohammed; it was Abraham. Abraham took Mohammed into Paradise and there was a beautiful woman with red lips. Mohammed ask who she belonged to, for she was very attractive to him. She was Zayd. When he got back, Mohammed told her of this.

1271 When Gabriel took Mohammed to each of the heavens and asked permission to enter he had to say who he had brought and whether they had a mission. They would then say, "Allah grant him life, brother and friend." When Mohammed got to the seventh heaven his Lord gave him the duty of fifty prayers a day. When he returned past Moses, Moses asked him how many prayers Allah had given him. When Moses heard that it was fifty, he said, "Prayer is a weighty matter and your people are weak. Go back and ask your Lord to reduce the number for you and your community. Mohammed went back and got the number reduced to forty. When he passed Moses, the same conversation took place. And so on until Allah reduced the number to five. Moses tried to get Mohammed to go back and get the number reduced even further, but Mohammed felt ashamed to ask for more.

In the Night Journey we see Mohammed as the successor to the Jewish prophets.

Islam defines the other religions.

> 7:163 *Ask them about the town that stood by the sea, how the Jews broke the Sabbath. Their fish came to them on their Sabbath day appearing on the surface of the water. But during the work week there were no fish to catch. So We made a trial of them for they were evildoers. And when some of them said, "Why do you preach to those whom Allah is about to destroy or chastise with awful doom?" They said, "To do our duty for the Lord so that they may be able to ward off evil."*

7:165 *When they disregarded the warnings that had been given to them [not to work on the Sabbath], We rescued those who had forbidden wrongdoing, and We punished the wrongdoers for their transgressions. But when they persisted in what they had been forbidden, We said to them, "Be as apes, despised and loathed." [The Jews were changed into apes.]*

1272 Mohammed continued to preach Islam and condemn the old Arabic religions. There were those of the Quraysh who defended their culture and religion and argued with him. Mohammed called them mockers and cursed one of them, "Oh Allah, blind him and kill his son." The Koran records the Meccan's political resistance as plots and schemes.

6:124 *So We have placed wicked ringleaders in every city to scheme there, but they only plot against themselves, and they do not realize it. And when a sign comes to them they say, "We will not believe until we receive one like those that Allah's messengers received." Allah knows best where to place His message. The unbelievers will be disgraced when they receive their punishment for their scheming.*

6:125 *For those whom Allah intends to guide, He will open their hearts to Islam. But for those whom He intends to mislead, He will make their hearts closed and hard, as though they had to climb up to the heavens. Thus does Allah penalize the unbelievers. And this is the right way of your Lord. We have detailed Our signs for those who will listen and see. They shall have an abode of peace with their Lord. He will be their protecting friend because of their works.*

7:194 *Those you call on besides Allah are His servants like you are. Call on them then, and let them answer you if you are truthful. Do they have feet to walk with? Do they have hands to hold with? Do they have eyes to see with? Do they have ears to hear with? Say: Call on these god-partners of yours. Then plot against me. Do not delay. My Lord is Allah who revealed the Scripture. He befriends the good. Whoever you call on besides Allah is not able to help you nor can they help themselves. If you call them to guidance, they will not hear you. You see them look towards you, but they do not see. Keep to forgiveness, command what is right, and turn away from the ignorant. And if a suggestion from Satan afflicts you, seek refuge with Allah. He hears and knows all things. Those who guard against evil when thoughts from Satan assault them remember Allah's guidance, and they see clearly. Their brethren plunge them deeper in error and do not cease in their efforts.*

7:203 *If you do not bring a revelation, they [the Meccans] say, "Why do you not have one?" Say: I only follow that which is inspired by my Lord These are clear proofs from your Lord and guidance and mercy for those who have faith. And when the Koran is read, listen to it with attention and hold your peace that mercy may be shown to you. Remember the Lord humbly within yourself in a low voice in the mornings and the evenings [prayer]. Do not be one of the neglectful ones. Those who are with the Lord are not too proud to serve Him. They celebrate His praises and prostrate themselves before Him.*

And if Mohammed were actually a prophet, why not show them something other than words. Why not do a miracle?

13:27 *The unbelievers say: Why does his Lord not send a sign down to him? Say: Allah will truly mislead whom he chooses and will guide to Himself those who turn to Him. They believe and their hearts find rest in remembering Allah. Without a doubt all hearts find rest in the remembrance of Allah. Those who believe and do what is right will be blessed and find joy in the end.*

13:40 *Whether We allow you to see the fulfillment of part of our threats or We cause you to die before it takes place, your part is only to spread the message while it is Our part to give out the punishment. Do they not recognize that We take control of their lands and invade its diminishing borders? When Allah makes a decree, nothing can be done to change it, and He is quick at His reckoning. Those who lived before them devised plots as well, but Allah is the master of all plotting. He knows every soul. The unbelievers will come to know for whom the heavenly home is destined. The unbelievers will say, "You are not a messenger of Allah." Say: Allah and whoever has knowledge of the Scriptures is a sufficient witness between you and me.*

If Judgment Day were to come, then the Meccans asked Mohammed to tell Allah to bring it here this day and prove Mohammed was a true prophet.

7:187 *They will ask you [Mohammed] about the fixed time of the final Hour. Say: That knowledge is only with my Lord. He alone will reveal it at its proper time. It weighs heavily on jinns and men. It will suddenly come to you. Say: The knowledge of it is only with Allah. Most men do not know.*
7:188 *Say: I have no power over any good or harm to myself except as Allah wills. If I had knowledge of his secrets, I would multiply the good, and evil would not touch me. I am only a warner, a bearer of glad tidings to those who believe.*

The Koran records the actual quotes of Mohammed's opponents.

41:26 *The unbelievers say, "Do not listen to this Koran. Instead speak during its reading so that you might gain the upper hand." But We will certainly give the unbelievers a taste of a terrible punishment, and We will repay them for their evil deeds. The reward of Allah's enemies is the*

Fire. The Fire will be their immortal home, a fitting reward for rejecting Our signs. And the unbelievers will say, "Lord, show us those jinn and men who misled us. We will crush them under our feet so that they become the lowest of all."

Mohammed continued to tell about older Arabian cultures that had refused to listen to their prophets. In every case, Allah smote them with a terrible scourge.

7:3 *Follow what has been revealed to you by the Lord, and do not follow any protectors beside Him. How little you remember. How many cities have We destroyed? We destroyed them as We raided them at night or while they slept in the afternoon. When Our wrath reached them, they could only reply, "Yes, we were wrongdoers."*
7:6 *Yes, We will call those to account to whom Our message has been sent. We will also question the messengers. And We will tell them their story with knowledge, as We have not been absent from them.*

1272 One day Mohammed stood with the angel, Gabriel, as the Quraysh performed the rituals of their religion. Among them were the leaders who defended their native culture and religion and opposed Mohammed. When the first leader passed by Gabriel, Gabriel threw a leaf in his face and blinded him. Gabriel then caused the second one to get dropsy which killed him. The third man Gabriel caused him to develop an infection which killed him. The fourth man was caused later to step on a thorn which killed him. Gabriel killed the last man who dared not to worship Allah with a brain disease.

MOHAMMED'S PROTECTOR AND WIFE BOTH DIE

1278 Mohammed's protector was his uncle, Abu Talib. When Abu Talib fell ill, some of the leaders of the Quraysh came to his bedside. They said to him, "You are one of our leaders and are near dying. Why don't you call Mohammed and let's see if we can't work out some solution to the pain and division in our tribe? Why doesn't he leave us alone, not bother us and we will not bother him? We will have our religion and he can have his."

1278 So Abu Talib called Mohammed to his side. "Nephew, these men have come so that you can give them something and they can give you something." Mohammed said, "If they will give me one word, they can rule the Persians and the Arabs. And they must accept Allah as their Lord and renounce their gods."

1278 The Quraysh said, "He will give us no agreement. Let Allah judge between us." And they left.

1278 Mohammed turned his attention to his dying uncle. He asked him to become a Muslim and then Mohammed could intercede for him on judgment day. His uncle told him, "The Quraysh would say that I only accept Islam because I fear death. But I should say it just to give you pleasure." He drifted off, but as he died, his lips moved. His brother put his head close to Abu Talib and listened. He then said, "Nephew, my brother said what you wished him to say." Mohammed's reply was, "I did not hear him." Mohammed left.

Abu Talib had taken the orphan Mohammed into his home and raised him. He took Mohammed on caravan trading missions to Syria and taught him how to be a businessman. Abu Talib was the clan chief who protected Mohammed's life when the rest of Mecca wanted to harm him. Abu Talib was Mohammed's life and security, but he was damned to Hell, he was not a Muslim and no amount of friendship could prevent that.

After Abu Talib's death, the pressure on Mohammed was greater. It reached the point where one of the Quraysh threw dust at Mohammed. This was the worst that happened.

The death of his wife had no political effect, but it was a blow to Mohammed. His wife was his chief confidant, and she consoled him.

MARRIAGE

M113[1] About three months after the death of Khadija Mohammed married Sauda, a widow and a Muslim.

M113 Abu Bakr had a daughter, Aisha, who was six years old. Soon after marrying Sauda Mohammed was betrothed to Aisha, who was to become his favorite wife. The consummation would not take place until she turned nine.

> M031, 5977[2] *Aisha reported Mohammed having said: I saw you in a dream for three nights when an angel brought you to me in a silk cloth and he said: Here is your wife, and when I removed (the cloth) from your face, lo, it was yourself, so I said: If this is from Allah, let Him carry it out.*

---

1. The M refers to the page of Sir William Muir's *The Life of Muhammad.*
2. An M reference with a comma is Muslim's Hadith, *Sahih Muslim.*

POLITICAL BEGINNINGS

CHAPTER 5

24:52 It is such as obey Allah and His Apostle, and fear
Allah and do right, that will win (in the end).

- Islam seeks political allies.
- Islam is not just a religion, but a political system.
- Immigration is a political act.
- When Islam has enough strength, it will use blood oaths and seek war against its hosts and others who oppose it.

Mohammed began to seek political allies. He began a political alliance with the new Muslims from Medina, a nearby town. Formal pledges were made that recognized Mohammed as a political leader.

Plans began to be made to leave Mecca and immigrate to Medina.

I279 With Abu Talib's death, Mohammed needed political allies. Mohammed went to the city of Taif, about fifty miles away, with one servant. In Taif he met with three brothers who were politically powerful. Mohammed called them to Islam and asked them to help him in his struggles with those who would defend their native religions.

I279 One brother said that if Mohammed were the representative of Allah, then the brother would go and rip off the covering of the Kabah, Allah's shrine.

I279 The second brother said, "Couldn't Allah have found someone better than Mohammed to be a prophet?"

I279 The third brother said, "Don't let me even speak to you. If you are the prophet of Allah as you say you are, then you are too important for me to speak with. And if you are not, then you are lying. And it is not right to speak with liars."

I280 Since they could not agree, Mohammed asked them to keep their meeting private. But Taif was a small town and within days everyone knew of Mohammed's presence. Taif was a very religious town in the old ways of the Arabs. Mohammed kept condemning them and their kind, until one day a mob gathered and drove him out of town, pelting him with stones.

The Koran frequently uses the imagery of slavery.

> 30:28 *He gave you a parable that relates to yourselves: Do you equally share your wealth with any slave you own? Would you fear your slave as you would fear a free man? This is how We explain Our signs to those who understand. No, you do not. The wicked, without knowledge, pursue their base desires. But who can guide those whom Allah has allowed to go astray? There will be no one to help them.*

> 16:71 *Allah has given more of His gifts of material things to some rather than others. In the same manner, those who have more do not give an equal share to their slaves so that they would share equally. Would they then deny the favors of Allah?*
> 16:75 *Allah gives you a parable. One man is a slave to another; he has no power. Another man has received many favors from Allah, and he spends from his wealth secretly and openly. Are the two men equal? Praise be to Allah. However, most do not understand. Allah gives another parable of two men. One man is dumb with no power. He is a tiresome burden to his master; no good comes from anything he is directed to do. Is he equal to the man who commands justice and walks the right path?*

> 39:29 *Allah sets forth a parable: "There is a slave who belongs to several partners and another slave owned by one man. Are the two in like circumstances?" No, Praise be to Allah. But most of them do not know.*

THE BEGINNING OF POWER AND JIHAD IN MEDINA

Medina was about a ten-day journey from Mecca, but since ancient times the Medinans had come to Mecca for the fairs. Medina was half Jewish and half Arabian, and there was an ongoing tension between the two. The Jews worked as farmers and craftsmen and were literate. They were the wealthy class, but their power was slowly waning. In times past the Arabs had raided and stolen from the Jews who retaliated by saying that one day a prophet would come and lead them to victory over the Arabs. In spite of the tensions, the Arab tribe of Khazraj were allies with them.

I286 So when the members of the Khazraj met Mohammed, they said among themselves, "This is the prophet the Jews spoke of. Let us join ranks with him before the Jews do." They became Muslims, and their tribe was rancorous and divided. They hoped that Islam could unite them, and soon every house in Medina had heard of Islam.

1289 The next year when the Medinan Muslims returned to Mecca, they took an oath to Mohammed. They returned to Medina, and soon many of Medinans submitted to Islam.

1294 At the next fair in Mecca, many of the new Muslims from Medina showed up. During the early part of the night about seventy of them left the caravan to meet with Mohammed. He recited the Koran and said, "I invite your allegiance on the basis that you protect me as you would your children." The Medinans gave their oath. After the oath, one of them asked about their now severed ties to the Jews of Medina. If they helped Mohammed with arms and they were successful would he go back to Mecca? Mohammed smiled and said, "No, blood is blood, and blood not to be paid for is blood not to be paid for." Blood revenge and its obligation were common to them. "I will war against them that war against you and be at peace with those at peace with you."

1299 One of the Medinans said to those who made the pledge, "Do you realize to what your are committing yourselves in pledging your support to this man? It is war against all. If you think that if you lose your property and your best are killed, and then you would give him up, then quit now. But if you think that you will be loyal to your oath if you lose your property and your best are killed, then take him, for it will profit you now and in Paradise." They asked what they would receive for their oath, Mohammed promised them Paradise. They all shook hands on the deal.

1301 In the morning the leaders of the Quraysh came to the caravan. They had heard that the Medinans had come to invite Mohammed to Medina and had pledged themselves to war against the Quraysh. The Quraysh wanted no part of war with the Medinans. Those Medinans in the caravan who were not Muslims were puzzled by all of this since they had no idea about the pledge in the night.

The Koran is very clear that the proper relationship between humanity and Allah is fear.

> 39:10 *Say: Oh, My servants who believe, fear your Lord. For those who do good in this world, good awaits. Allah's earth is spacious. Those who are patient will be rewarded in full measure.*
>
> 39:11 *Say: I am commanded that I serve Allah with sincere devotion. I am commanded to be the first of those who submit. Say: If I should disobey my Lord, I fear the penalty of a grievous day. Say: I serve Allah being sincere in my obedience.*
>
> 39:15 *Worship what you will besides Him. Say: The losers will be those who will lose their own souls and their families on the day of resurrection. Surely, this is a clear loss. They will be covered by Fire from above and below. With this Allah stirs fear in His servants, so fear Me, My servants.*

BACK IN MEDINA

1304 Back in Medina the Muslims now practiced their new religion openly. But most of the Arabs still practiced their ancient tribal religions. The Muslims would desecrate the old shrines and ritual objects. They would even break into houses and steal the ritual objects and throw them into the latrines. On one occasion they killed a dog and tied the dog's body to the ritual object and thew it into the latrine.

THE OPENING WORDS OF WAR

1313 Up to now the main tension in the division in the Quraysh tribe over the new religion had been resolved by words. Curses and insults had been exchanged. Mohammed condemned the ancient religion and customs on an almost daily basis. The Quraysh had mocked Mohammed and abused lower class converts. What blood had been drawn had been in the equivalent of a brawl. Dust had been thrown, but no real violence. No one had died.

IMMIGRATION

1314 The Muslim Medinans had pledged Mohammed support in war and to help the Muslims from Mecca. The Muslims in Mecca left and went to Medina. The Muslims from both Mecca and Medina were about to be tested.

MEDINA

POLITICAL POWER

CHAPTER 6

8:46 Obey Allah and His messenger, and do not argue
with one another for fear that you will lose courage and
strength. Be patient for Allah is with the patient.

- Legal and moral dualism (treating Muslims and non-Muslims differently) is a fundamental principle of political Islam.

Mohammed was the last of the Muslims to leave Mecca for Medina. In Medina he set up a political charter which established a dualistic legal and ethical system. He then consummated his marriage to Aisha when she was nine years old.

I324-326 All of the Muslims, except for Mohammed, Ali and Abu Bakr, had left for Medina. The Quraysh saw that Mohammed had new allies outside of Mecca and their influence. They feared that Mohammed would join them and they knew that his oath of allegiance included war with the Quraysh and Mecca. So the Quraysh assembled as a council in order to figure out what to do. In the end the Quraysh let them go. The Quraysh wanted the their problem to go away.

8:30 *Remember the unbelievers who plotted against you and sought to have you taken prisoner or to have you killed or banished. They made plans, as did Allah, but Allah is the best plotter of all.*
8:31 *When Our revelations are told to them they say, "We have heard them before, and if we wanted to, we could say the same kinds of things. They are nothing but the fables of old." And then they said, "Allah! If this is indeed the truth sent down from You, then send down a shower of stones upon our heads or some other terrible punishment." But Allah would not punish them while you were there with them. He would not punish them if they asked to be forgiven. Nevertheless, Allah would be justified in punishing them because they have prevented the believers from entering the Sacred Mosque, even though they have no right to guard it. The Allah-fearing are its only guardians although most of them do not realize it. Their prayers at the Sacred House are nothing*

*more significant than whistling or clapping hands to Allah. "Taste your
punishment for your disbelief."*
8:36 *The unbelievers spend their wealth with the intent to turn others
away from Allah's path. In this way they drain their wealth, but they will
regret it, and they will be conquered in the end. The unbelievers will be
driven into Hell. Allah will divide the bad from the good. He will take the
wicked, pile them on top of one another, and cast them into Hell; truly
they are the losers.*

1336-337 In Medina Mohammed set to work building the first mosque.
There were now two groups of Muslims in Medina, the Quraysh Immi-
grants from Mecca and the Helpers from Medina.

THE COVENANT

1341 Mohammed wrote up a charter or covenant for a basis of law and
government. The religion of Islam now had a political system. Islam now
had power over those outside the mosque. All Muslims, whether from
Mecca, Medina or anywhere else, were part of a community, *umma,* that
excluded others. There was one set of ethics for the Muslims and another
set for the non-Muslims. Duality was established as a fundamental principle of Islamic ethics.

1341 Muslims should oppose any who would sow discord among other
Muslims. A Muslim should not kill another Muslim, nor should he help a
non-Muslim against a Muslim. Muslims are friends to each other, to the
exclusion of non-Muslims. Muslims shall avenge blood shed of another
Muslim in jihad. A non-believer shall not intervene against a Muslim.

1342 The Jews who align themselves with Mohammed are to be treated
fairly. Jews are to help pay for war if they are fighting with the Muslims
as allies. No Jew may go to war without the permission of Mohammed,
except for revenge killings. Jews must help Muslims if they are attacked.
All trouble and controversy must be judged by Mohammed. No Meccans
are to be aided.

MARRIAGE

M177 About seven months after arriving in Medina Mohammed, aged
fifty-three, consummated his marriage with Aisha, now age nine. She
moved out of her father's house into what was to become a compound of
apartments adjoining the mosque. She was allowed to bring her dolls into
the harem due to her age.

THE HYPOCRITES

CHAPTER 7

47:33 Believers! Obey Allah and the messenger,
and do not let your effort be in vain.

- No criticism of Islam is allowed.
- Islam makes political and physical threats of violence against those who cause trouble against Islam.
- Humor about Islam or Mohammed is forbidden.
- Commitment to Islam and jihad must be absolute.

Some of the Medinans submitted to Islam and then had doubts. Those who doubted were called hypocrites, and the Koran began to devote attention to those who were less than totally committed to Mohammed. The smallest comment of doubt or humor could bring the full attention of Islam to bear.

The Koran moves from threatening punishment for unbelievers in Hell to political punishment now. Many of the Medinans argued against Mohammed and defended their religions.

THE HYPOCRITES

1351 Before Mohammed arrived, the Arabs who practiced their ancient religions were content with their religion and tolerant of others. Many Arabs became Muslims due to a pressure to join Islam. But in secret they were hypocrites who allied themselves with the Jews because they thought Mohammed was deluded.

1365 The Koran about the hypocrites:

> 2:8 *And some of the people [the Jews] say, "We believe in Allah and the Day," although they do not really believe. They wish to deceive Allah and His believers, but they fool no one but themselves although they do not know it. Their hearts are diseased, and Allah has increased their suffering. They will suffer an excruciating doom because of their lies.*

1355 One of the Medinans became a Muslim and later began to doubt the truth of Mohammed and said, "If this man is right, we are worse than donkeys." His best friend had converted and told Mohammed of his friend's doubts. Allegiance to Islam comes before family, nation, or friend. When Mohammed confronted him about his remarks and doubts, he denied it. The Koran's comments:

> 9:74 *They swear by Allah that they said nothing wrong, yet they spoke blasphemy, and some Muslims became unbelievers. They planned what they could not carry out [a plan against Mohammed], and only disapproved of it because Allah and His Messenger had enriched them by His bounty [the resistance to Mohammed decreased when the money from the spoils of war came into the Medinan economy]. If they repent, it will be better for them, but if they fall back into their sin, Allah will afflict them with a painful doom in this world and the next. On earth, they will have neither friend nor protector.*

1356 Ironically, the friend who reported the doubts to Mohammed later turned against him, killed two Muslims during battle, and fled to Mecca. Mohammed ordered him killed, but he escaped.

1357 Mohammed used to say about one of the hypocrites that he had the same face as Satan. The man used to sit and listen to Mohammed and then take back to the hypocrites what he said. He said of Mohammed, "Mohammed is all ears. If anyone tells him anything, he will believe it." The Koran speaks of him and other hypocrites:

> 9:61 *There are some of them who injure the Messenger and say, "He is only a hearer." Say: He is a hearer of good for you. He believes in Allah and believes in the faithful. He is a mercy to those of you who believe, but those who injure the Messenger of Allah will suffer a painful doom. They swear to you by Allah to please you, but Allah and His Messenger are worthier, so they should please Him if they are believers.*
> 9:63 *Do they not know that whoever opposes Allah and His Messenger will abide in the Fire of Hell, where they will remain forever? This is the great shame.*

1358 One of the hypocrites excused his criticism by saying that he was only talking and jesting. No criticism was too small to be unnoticed.

> 9:65 *If you ask them, they will surely say, "We were only talking idly and jesting." Say: Do you mock Allah, His signs, and His Messenger? Make no excuse. You have rejected faith after you accepted it. If we forgive some of you, we will punish others because they are evildoers. Hypocritical men and women have an understanding with one another. They command what is evil, forbid what is just, and do not pay the poor tax. They have*

forgotten Allah, and He has forgotten them. The hypocrites are the rebellious wrongdoers. Allah promises the hypocritical men and women and the unbelievers the Fire of Hell, and they will abide there; it is enough for them. Allah has cursed them, and an eternal torment will be theirs.

1365 The hypocrites change their faces depending upon who they are with. When they are with the Muslims, they believe. But when they are with the evil ones (the Jews) they say they are with the Jews. It is the Jews who order them to deny the truth and contradict Mohammed.

33:60 *If the hypocrites, the men with diseased hearts and the troublemakers in Medina, do not desist, We will raise you up against them and they will not remain in the city much longer. They will be cursed, and wherever they are found, they will be seized and murdered. It was Allah's same practice with those who came before them, and you will find no change in Allah's ways.*

4:113 *If it had not been for Allah's grace and mercy, a group of them [hypocrites] would have certainly plotted to mislead you. They have only succeeded in leading themselves astray, and they cannot harm you. Allah has sent His Scripture and wisdom to you and has taught you things you did not know before. Allah's grace toward you has been great. There is nothing good in most of their secret conversations except that which commands charity, goodness, and peace among the people. Whoever does this to please Allah, We will give them a rich reward.*

4:115 *Anyone who opposes the Messenger after having received Our guidance and follows a path other than that of the true believer will be left to their own devices. We will lead them into Hell, an evil home.*

THE JEWS

CHAPTER 8

*9:63 Do they not know that whoever opposes Allah
and His Messenger will abide in the Fire of Hell, where
they will remain forever? This is the great shame.*

- Jews and Christians must acknowledge the truth of what Mohammed says.
- Jews are special enemies of Islam.

The Jews comprised about half of Medina. In Mecca Mohammed claimed the mantle of the Jewish tradition of being a prophet. But the Jews in Medina said that Mohammed was not a prophet. Then Mohammed claimed that the Jews were corrupt and that only he knew the actual doctrine of the Jewish scriptures.

Now the Koran and Mohammed began to attack the Jews and the direction of Islamic prayer was changed from Jerusalem to Mecca.

When Mohammed came to Medina about half the town were Jews. There were three tribes of Jews and two tribes of Arabs. Almost none of the Jews had Hebrew names. They were Arabs to some degree. At the same time many of the Arabs' religious practice had elements of Judaism. The Jews were farmers and tradesmen and lived in their own fortified quarters. In general they were better educated and more prosperous than the Arabs.

Before Mohammed arrived, there had been bad blood and killing among the tribes. The last battle had been fought by the two Arab tribes, but each of the Jewish tribes had joined the battle with their particular Arab allies. In addition to that tension between the two Arab tribes, there was a tension between the Jews and the Arabs. The division of the Jews and fighting on different sides was condemned by Mohammed. The Torah preached that the Jews should be unified, and they failed in this.

All of these quarrelsome tribal relationships were one reason that Mohammed was invited to Medina. But the result was further polarization, not unity. The new split was between Islam and those Arabs and their Jewish partners who resisted Islam.

1351 About this time, the leaders of the Jews spoke out against Mohammed. The rabbis began to ask him difficult questions. Doubts and questions about his doctrine were about Allah. Doubts about Allah were evil. However, two of the Jewish Arabs joined with Mohammed as Muslims. They believed him when he said that he was the Jewish prophet that came to fulfill the Torah.

THE REAL TORAH IS IN THE KORAN

Mohammed said repeatedly that the Jews and Christians corrupted their sacred texts in order to conceal the fact that he was prophesied in their scriptures. The stories in the Koran are similar to those of the Jew's scriptures, but they make different points. In the Koran, all of the stories found in Jewish scripture indicated that Allah destroyed those cultures that did not listen to their messengers. According to Mohammed, the scriptures of the Jews have been changed to hide the fact that Islam is the true religion.

1364 But the Jews did not believe that Mohammed was a prophet. As a result, they are in error and cursed by Allah. And by denying his prophethood they conspired against him and Islam.

1367 Mohammed is the final prophet. His coming was in the original Torah. Allah has blessed the Jews and protected them and now they refuse to believe the final and ideal prophet. The Jews are not ignorant, but deceitful. The Jews know the truth of Mohammed and cover the truth and hide the truth with lies.

1367 The Koran repeats the many favors that Allah has done for the Jews—they were the chosen people, delivered from slavery under the pharaoh, given the sacred Torah and all they have ever done is to sin. They have been forgiven many times by Allah, and still, they are as hard as rocks and refuse to believe Mohammed. They have perverted the Torah after understanding it.

> 2:75 *Can you believers then hope that the Jews will believe you even though they heard the Word of Allah and purposefully altered it [Mohammed said the Jews hid their scriptures that foretold Mohammed would be the final prophet] after they understood its meaning? And when they are among the believers they say, "We believe too," but when they are alone with one another they say, "Will you tell them what Allah has revealed to you so that they can argue with you about it in the presence of your*

Lord?" Do you not have any sense? Do they not realize that Allah knows what they hide as well as what they reveal?

1369 The Jews' sins are so great that Allah has changed them into apes. Still they will not learn and refuse to admit that Mohammed is their prophet. They know full well the truth and hide and confuse others. Even when they say to Mohammed they believe, they conceal their resistance.

> 2:88 *They say, "Our hearts are hardened." But Allah has cursed them for their unbelief. Their faith is weak. And when the Scriptures came from Allah, confirming what they already had, they refused to believe in it, although they had long prayed for victory over the unbelievers. Therefore, Allah's curse is on those without faith! They have sold themselves for a vile price by not believing what Allah has sent down, begrudging Him the right to send it to whichever messenger He pleases. They have brought relentless wrath upon themselves. Disgraceful punishment awaits the unbelievers.*
>
> 2:91 *When they are told, "Believe in what Allah has sent down," they say, "We believe in what was sent down to us." They reject what has since been sent down even though it is true and confirms their own scriptures. Say: Then why did you kill the messengers of Allah in the past if you are truly believers?*

1370 The Jews have understood the truth of Mohammed and then changed their scriptures to avoid admitting that Mohammed is right.

> 2:174 *Those [the Jews] who conceal any part of the Scriptures which Allah has revealed in order to gain a small profit shall ingest nothing but Fire in their stomachs. Allah will not speak to them on the Day of Resurrection, and they will pay a painful penalty. They are the ones who buy error at the price of guidance and torture at the price of forgiveness; how intently they seek the Fire!*

MOHAMMED TRULY FOLLOWS THE RELIGION OF ABRAHAM

1381 Christians and Jews argued with Mohammed that if he wished to have salvation, then he would have to convert. But Mohammed is the one who truly follows the religion of Abraham. Mohammed is the true Jew with the true Torah.

1383 Mohammed entered a Jewish school and called the Jews to Islam. One asked him, "What is your religion, Mohammed?"

"The religion of Abraham."

"But Abraham was a Jew."

"Then let the Torah judge between us." He meant the Torah of the Koran.

3:66 *Abraham was neither a Jew nor a Christian, but a righteous man, a Muslim, not an idol worshipper. Doubtless the ones who follow Abraham are the closest to him, along with this messenger and the believers. Allah is protector of the faithful. Some of the People of the Book try to lead you astray, but they only mislead themselves, although they may not realize it.*

3:70 *People of the Book [Jews and Christians]! Why do you reject Allah's revelations when you have witnessed their truth? People of the Book! Why do you cover up the truth with lies when you know that you hide the truth?*

1397 Three Jews came to Mohammed and said, "Do you not allege that you follow the religion of Abraham and believe in the Torah which we have and testify that it is the truth from Allah?" He replied, "Certainly, but you have sinned and broken the covenant contained therein and concealed what you were ordered to make plain to men. I disassociate myself from your sin [the Jew's altering the part of the Torah that prophesied the coming of Ahmed (a variation of the name Mohammed)]".

AN OMINOUS CHANGE

1381 In Mecca Mohammed spoke well of the Jews, who were very few. In Medina there were many Jews and his relations were tense. Up to now Mohammed had lead prayer in the direction of Jerusalem. Now the *kiblah*, direction of prayer, was changed to the Kabah in Mecca. Some of the Jews came to him and asked why he had changed the direction of prayer. After all, he said that he followed the religion of Abraham. The Koran responded:

2:142 *The foolish ones will say, "What makes them turn from the kiblah [the direction they faced during Islamic prayer]?" Say: Both the east and the west belong to Allah. He will guide whom He likes to the right path. We have made you [Muslims] the best of nations so that you can be witnesses over the world and so that the messenger may be a witness for you. We appointed the former kiblah towards Jerusalem and now Mecca so that We could identify the messenger's true followers and those who would turn their backs on him. It was truly a hard test, but not for those whom Allah guided. It was not Allah's purpose that your faith should be in vain, for Allah is full of pity and merciful toward mankind. We have seen you [Mohammed] turn your face to every part of Heaven for guidance, and now We will have you turn to a kiblah that pleases you. So turn your face towards the direction of the sacred Mosque, and wherever the believers are, they will turn their faces toward it. The People of the Book know that this is the truth from their Lord, and Allah is not unaware of*

what they do. Even if you were to give the People of the Book [Jews] ev-
ery sign, they would not accept your kiblah, nor would you accept theirs.
None of them will accept the kiblah of the others. If you should follow
their way after receiving the knowledge you possess, then you will cer-
tainly be a part of the unrighteous.

Since Islam is the successor to Judaism, Allah was the successor to Je-
hovah. It was actually Allah who had been the deity of the Jews and the
Jews had deliberately hidden this fact by corrupted scriptures. For this the
Jews will be cursed.

2:159 *Those who conceal the clear signs and guidance [Mohammed said*
that the Jews corrupted the Scriptures that predicted his prophecy] that
We have sent down after We have made them clear in the Scriptures for
mankind, will receive Allah's curse and the curse of those who damn
them. But for those who repent, change their ways, and proclaim the
truth, I will relent. I am relenting and merciful. Those who reject Me and
die unbelievers will receive the curse of Allah and of the angels and of
mankind. They will remain under the curse forever with no lightening of
their punishment and no reprieve. Your Allah is the one god. There is no
god but Him. He is compassionate and merciful.

4:47 *To those of you [Jews and Christians] to whom the Scriptures were*
given: Believe in what We have sent down confirming the Scriptures you
already possess before We destroy your faces and twist your heads around
backwards, or curse you as We did those [the Jews] who broke the Sab-
bath for Allah's commandments will be carried out.

THE CHRISTIANS

CHAPTER 9

33:21 You have an excellent example in Allah's Messenger
for those of you who put your hope in Allah and the
Last Day and who praise Allah continually.

- There is no Trinity. Jesus was another prophet of Allah.
- Christ did not die on the cross.
- Only those Christians who acknowledge the truth of Mohammed are actually Christians.
- Islam defines what all religions are.
- Jews are special enemies of Islam.

Christ was a prophet of Allah and a Muslim. Christ comes from Allah. He was not crucified. Those who insist that Jesus was the Son of God will burn in Hell.

1404 While some Christians were in Medina, they argued religion with Mohammed. They held forth with the doctrine of the Trinity and the divinity of Christ. Mohammed later laid out the Islamic doctrine of the Christian doctrine. The Koran tells in detail the "real" story of Jesus, who is just another of Allah's prophets, and that the Trinity of the Christians is Allah, Jesus and Mary.

1406 No one has power except through Allah. Allah gave the prophet Jesus the power of raising the dead, healing the sick, making birds of clay and having them fly away. Allah gave Jesus these signs as a mark of his being a prophet. But Allah did not give the powers of appointing kings, the ability to change night to day. These lacks of power show that Jesus was a man, not part of a Trinity. If he were part of God, then all powers would have been in his command. Then he would not have to have been under the dominion of kings.

1407-8 Christ spoke in the cradle and then spoke to men as a grown man. Speaking from the cradle is a sign of his being a prophet. Christ's prophethood was confirmed by making clay birds fly. By Allah Christ healed the blind, the lepers, and raised the dead.

> 5:109 *One day Allah will assemble the messengers and say, "What response did you receive from mankind?" They will say, "We have no knowledge. You are the knower of secrets." Then Allah will say, "Oh Jesus, Son of Mary, remember my favor to you and your mother when I strengthened you with the Holy Spirit [Gabriel] so that you would speak to men alike in childhood and when grown. I taught you the Scripture, wisdom, the Torah, and the Gospel, and you created the figure of a bird with clay, by my permission, and breathed into it. With My permission it became a bird. You also healed the blind and the leper, with My permission. With My permission you raised the dead. I restrained the Children of Israel from harming you when you went to them with clear signs, and the un-believers said, "This is nothing but plain sorcery."*
> 5:111 *When I revealed to the disciples, "Believe in Me and the One I sent," they said, "We believe and bear witness to You that we are Muslims."*

1408 Christ only comes through Allah. Christ's signs of being a proph-et come only from Allah. Jesus enjoins others to worship Allah, not him. But people refused to hear him, the Disciples came forth to help him with his mission. The Disciples were servants of Allah and were Muslims just like Christ.

1409 Christ was not crucified. When the Jews plotted against Christ, they found Allah to be the best plotter. Allah took Jesus up directly to him and will refute those who say he was crucified and was resurrected. On the final day, the Day of Resurrection, those who follow Christ but do not believe in his divinity will be blessed. Those who insist that Christ is God, part of the Trinity, and reject true faith will be punished in Hell.

> 3:54 *So the Jews plotted and Allah plotted, but Allah is the best of plotters. And Allah said, "Jesus! I am going to end your life on earth and lift you up to Me. [Jesus did not die on the cross. He was taken to Allah. He will return to kill the anti-Christ and then die a natural death.] I will send the unbelievers away from you and lift up those who believe above all others until the Day of Resurrection. Then all will return to Me and I will judge their disputes. As for the unbelievers, they will be punished with excruciating agony in this world and the world to come. They will have no one to help them. As for the believers who do good works, He will fully reward them. Allah does not love those who do wrong. These signs and this wise warning We bring to you."*

Although the Koran says less about Christians than Jews, it does ad-dress them.

61:6 *And remember when Jesus, son of Mary, said, "Children of Israel! I am Allah's messenger sent to confirm the Law which was already revealed to you and to bring good news of a messenger who will come after me whose name will be Ahmad." [Ahmad was one of Mohammed's names. This quote of Jesus is not found in any Christian scriptures.] Yet when he [Mohammed] came to them with clear signs, they said, "This is merely sorcery!" And who is more evil than the one who, when called to submit to Islam, makes up a lie about Allah? Allah does not guide the evil-doers! They wish to put out Allah's light with their mouths, but as much as the unbelievers hate it, Allah will perfect His light.*

61:9 *It is He who has sent forth His messenger with guidance and the true religion so that, though the idolaters hate it, He will make His religion victorious over all the others.*

The unbelievers, the Christians, Jews and pagans will burn forever in the fire of Hell.

98:6 *The unbelievers among the People of the Book and the idolaters will burn for eternity in the Fire of Hell. Of all the created beings, they are the most despicable. As for those who believe and do good works, they are the most noble of all created beings.*

Allah changes His revelations when needed.

2:106 *Whatever of Our revelations We repeal or cause to be forgotten, We will replace with something superior or comparable. [There are as many as 225 verses of the Koran that are altered by later verses. This is called abrogation.] Do you not know that Allah has power over all things? Do you not know that Allah reigns sovereign over the heavens and earth and besides Him you have no protector or helper?*

16:101 *When We exchange one verse for another, and Allah knows best what He reveals, they say, "You are making this up." Most of them do not understand.*

JIHAD, WAR AGAINST ALL

CHAPTER 10

*4:42 On that day, the unbelievers and those who disobeyed
the Messenger will wish they could sink into the earth
for they cannot hide a single thing from Allah.*

- Islam uses a progression of force. In the beginning, Islam claims that it is a better member of the host community. Then Islam argues, pressures, and threatens. Finally, when it is strong enough, it uses armed violence at a tactical level.
- Jihad, the struggle in Allah's cause, is a sacred method of political persuasion.
- All jihad is defensive since resisting Islam is an offense to Allah.
- Immigration is the first stage of jihad.
- Jihad does not fight by the rules of the host community.
- Deceit and sneak attacks are part of jihad.
- Mohammed is the ideal jihadist. His acts are the basis for every tactic and strategy of Islam.
- When small acts of violence and theft work well, Islam commits to larger acts of violence. The first level of violent jihad is crime.
- The killing of nonbelievers is a joyful, sacred act.
- Jihad uses torture of non-Muslims for the benefit of Islam.
- Jihad takes wealth from the non-Muslims by force.
- Killing prisoners-of-war is acceptable in jihad.
- A jihadist is superior to an ordinary Muslim.
- Battle follows battle. Jihad is unceasing.

After a year in Medina, Islam had matured as a political system. Mohammed sent his armed men out to attack the caravans of his old enemies, the Meccans.

On their eighth attempt, the Muslims were successful in using deceit to attack a caravan in a sacred month. The Meccans had offended Islam and the traditional rules of war did not apply to

Islam's enemies. Mohammed distributed the stolen goods to his followers.

The Meccan caravan was due to pass near Medina, and Mohammed decided to strike his enemies and raid it. But the caravan leader was fearful and sent a fast rider to Mecca for armed help. Mohammed's army and the Meccan fighters camped near Badr.

Every warrior who died was promised Paradise. Mohammed gave the order and the battle started. The Muslims were outnumbered, but fought with courage. Islam was triumphant and some of Mohammed's old enemies were killed.

The victory and the killing of the nonbelievers was a joy to Allah. Indeed, Allah sent angels to help with the killing. The new path of Islam was given in the Koran. War was instituted as a permanent strategy of Islamic politics. The spoils of war were made sacred. Part of the wealth taken in jihad was to be used to pay the warriors. One fifth of the booty went to Mohammed.

Immediately after winning at Badr, Mohammed sent out warriors on other raids. The new foreign policy of constant, sacred war was in place.

In Mecca, Mohammed had divided the community into Islam and those of the native Arabic religions. In Mecca he adopted all the classical Jewish stories to prove his prophesy and spoke well of the Jews. But there were almost no Jews living in Mecca, and therefore, no one to differ with him.

In Medina half of the population were Jews, who let Mohammed know that they disagreed with him. So in Medina, Mohammed argued with Jews as well as the non-Muslim Arabs. Even though there were very few in the town who were Christian, Mohammed argued against them as well. All non-Muslims were verbally attacked in Medina.

I415 It was thirteen years after he started preaching and one to two years after going to Medina that Mohammed prepared for war as commanded by Allah. He would fight his enemies, those who were not Muslims.

THE FIRST RAIDS

I416-423 Mohammed sent forth his fighters on seven armed raids to find the trade caravans headed to Mecca.

JIHAD—THE FIRST KILLING

1423-4 Mohammed sent Abdullah out with eight men. A caravan of the Quraysh passed by the Muslims as they overlooked the road from a rise. The caravan was loaded with leather and raisins. When the Quraysh saw them they were scared because they had slept not too far from here, but one of the Muslims had a shaved head. Now a shaved head was a mark of pilgrim so the Quraysh felt better. They were safe. They were also in a sacred month when weapons were not carried.

1425 The Muslims took council. They were in a dilemma. If they attacked the caravan now, they would be killing in a sacred month. Luckily, the sacred month ended today and tomorrow there would be no taboo about killing. But there was another problem. By tonight they would be in the sacred area of Mecca. In the sanctified area, there could never be any killing. They hesitated and talked about what to do. They decided to go ahead and kill as many as possible today and take their goods.

1425 Islam drew first blood against the Quraysh of Mecca. They attacked the unarmed men. Amr was killed by an arrow. He was the first man to be killed in jihad. One man escaped and they captured two prisoners. They took their camels with their goods and headed back to Mohammed in Medina. On the way they talked about how Mohammed would get one fifth of the stolen goods, spoils.

1425 When they got back, Mohammed said that he did not order them to attack in the sacred month. So he held the caravan and the two prisoners in suspense and refused to do anything with the goods or prisoners. The prisoners said, "Mohammed has violated the sacred month, shed blood therein, stolen goods and taken prisoners." But the Koran said:

> 2:216 *You are commanded to fight although you dislike it. You may hate something that is good for you, and love something that is bad for you. Allah knows and you do not. When they ask you about fighting in the holy month, say: Fighting at this time is a serious offense, but it is worse in Allah's eyes to deny others the path to Him, to disbelieve in Him, and to drive His worshippers out of the Sacred Mosque. Idolatry is a greater sin than murder. They will not stop fighting you until you turn away from your religion. But any of you who renounce your faith and die an unbeliever, will have your works count for nothing in this world and the world to come. These people will be prisoners of the Fire, where they will live forever.*

> *You (Quraysh) count war in the holy month a grave matter*
> *But graver is your opposition to Mohammed and your unbelief.*

Though you defame us for killing Amr
Our lances drank Amr's blood
We lit the flame of war.   — *Abu Bakr, the first caliph*

1426 To resist the doctrine of Islam and to try and persuade Muslims to drop their faith is worse than killing. Before Islam, the rule of justice in Arabia was a killing for a killing, but now to resist Islam was worse than murder. Those who argue against Islam and resist Islam can be killed as a sacred act. The spoils were distributed and a ransom set for the prisoners. The men who had killed and stolen were now concerned as to whether they would get their take of the spoils. So once again the Koran spoke:

FIGHTING IN ALLAH'S CAUSE—BADR

1428 Mohammed heard that Abu Sufyan was coming with a large caravan of thirty to forty Quraysh from Syria. Mohammed called the Muslims together and said, "Go out and attack it, perhaps Allah will give us the prey."

1428 As the caravan approached Medina, Abu Sufyan became worried and questioned every rider on the road about Mohammed. Then he heard intelligence that indeed Mohammed was going to attack. He sent out a fast rider to Mecca for aid.

1433 Mohammed and his men headed out of Medina for what was to prove to be one of the most important battles in all of history, a battle that would change the world forever.

1435 Mohammed was cheered. He said, "I see the enemy dead on the ground." They headed towards Badr where they camped near there for the night. He sent several scouts to the well at Badr and the scouts found two slaves with water camels. They felt sure they were from the Quraysh caravan and brought back them back to Mohammed. Two of Mohammed's men questioned them as Mohammed was nearby praying. The men replied that they were from the Quraysh. Mohammed's men began to beat them and torture the slaves as Mohammed prayed.

1436 Mohammed told his men that the slaves told them the truth until they started to beat and torture them. Then the slaves had lied but it had been the lie that they wanted to hear. Mohammed asked the men how many of the Quraysh there were and who were the leaders of the Quraysh. When they told him he was delighted and told his warriors that Mecca had sent their best men to be slaughtered.

1439-440 Both armies had an idea of the location of the other. Mohammed went ahead to chose a place to camp and set up for battle on the morrow.

1440-444 The Quraysh marched forth at daybreak. The battle started.

1445 Some arrows flew and one Muslim was killed. Mohammed addressed his army. "By Allah, every man who is slain this day by fighting with courage and advancing, not retreating, will enter Paradise." One of his men had been eating dates said, "You mean that there is nothing between me and Paradise except being killed by the Quraysh?" He flung the dates to the side, picked up his sword and set out to fight. He got his wish and was killed later.

1445 One of Mohammed's men asked what makes Allah laugh? Mohammed answered, "When he plunges into the midst of the enemy without armor." The man removed his coat of mail, picked up his sword and made ready to attack.

1445 Now the two armies started to close ranks and move forward. Mohammed had said that his warriors were not to start until he gave the order. Now he took a handful of pebbles and threw them at the Quraysh and said, "Curse those faces." The Muslims advanced. The battle had begun.

1451 As the battle wound down, Mohammed issued orders for the fighters to be on the look out for Abu Jahl, the enemy of Allah, among the slain. He was found still fighting in a thicket. A Muslim made for him and cut off his lower leg. Another Muslim passed by him as Abu Jahl lay dying and put his foot on his neck. The Muslim said, "Has Allah put you to shame, enemy of Allah?" Abu Jahl gasped, "How has He shamed me? Am I any more remarkable than any other you have killed?" The Muslim cut off his head.

1452 He took the head back to Mohammed and said, "Here is the head of the enemy of Allah" and threw it at Mohammed's feet. The Prophet said, "Praise be to Allah."

1455 As the bodies were dragged to a well, one of the Muslims saw the body of his father thrown in. He said, "My father was a virtuous, wise, kind, and cultured man. I had hoped he would become a Muslim. He died an unbeliever." His abode is hellfire forever. Before Islam killing of kin and tribal brothers had been forbidden since the dawn of time. After Islam brother would kill brother and sons would kill their fathers. Fighting in Allah's cause—jihad.

1454 The bodies of the Quraysh were thrown into a well. The Apostle of Allah leaned over the well and shouted at the bodies, "Oh people of the well, have you found what Allah promised to be true?" The Muslims were puzzled by his question. Mohammed explained that the dead could hear him.

I456 Now it was time to take the property from the dead who could no longer claim what had been theirs. It was now the spoils of jihad and the profit of Islam. Mohammed divided it equally among all who were there. He took one fifth for himself.

> 8:1 *When they ask you about the spoils of war say: The spoils belong to Allah and His messenger. [This sura was written after the Battle of Badr.] Therefore, fear Allah and settle your arguments. Obey Allah and His messenger if you are truly believers.*

I459 Off they set for Medina with the spoils of war and the prisoners to be ransomed. Except for one prisoner, who had spoken against Mohammed. He was brought in front of the Prophet to be killed and before the sword struck, he asked, "Who will care for my family?"

M230 The Prophet replied, "Hell!" After he fell dead, Mohammed said, "Unbeliever in Allah and his Prophet and his Book! I give thanks to Allah who has killed you and made my eyes satisfied."

I476 After the battle of Badr there came about an entire sura of the Koran. The eighth chapter is called War Treasure or Booty and also the Spoils of War. The idea of the battle of Badr was Mohammed's. Many of the Muslims had no desire to go to war. The armed Muslims wanted to attack the caravan, not the army.

I477 The Muslims were not alone. No, Allah sent a thousand angels to help kill those who worshiped in the ancient ways and rituals. To resist Mohammed was a death sentence from Allah. When a Muslim meets a non-Muslim in war, they should never turn their backs, except as a tactical maneuver. A Muslim fighting in Allah's cause must face the enemy. To not do so brings on the wrath of Allah and the judgment of Hell.

> 8:5 *Remember how your Lord commanded you to leave your homes to fight for the truth, but some of the believers were opposed to it? They disputed the truth after you had revealed it, as if they were being led to certain death before their eyes.*
> 8:7 *And when Allah promised that you would defeat one of the two groups of enemies, you wished to attack the group that was defenseless. [Mohammed had started out to attack a large, unarmed Meccan caravan. But a thousand-man army from Mecca arrived to protect the caravan.] But Allah wished to justify the truth of His words and to cut the unbelievers down so that the truth would triumph and the lies would be shown false, much to the opposition of the guilty.*

8:9 *Remember when you begged your Lord for help and He said, "I will send the ranks of a thousand angels to your aid?" Allah gave this as a message of good news to bring them hope for victory only comes from Allah. Allah is mighty and wise.*

8:11 *Remember when sleep overcame you, a sign of His reassurance? He sent down rain from the heavens to make you clean and to rid you of the grime of Satan, to strengthen your hearts and steady your feet. [The rain before the battle muddied the ground and hindered the Meccan cavalry.]*

8:12 *Then your Lord spoke to His angels and said, "I will be with you. Give strength to the believers. I will send terror into the unbelievers' hearts, cut off their heads and even the tips of their fingers!" This was because they opposed Allah and His messenger. Ones who oppose Allah and His messenger will be severely punished by Allah. We said, "This is for you! Taste it and know that the unbelievers will receive the torment of the Fire."*

8:15 *Believers! When you meet the unbelievers marching into battle, do not turn your back to them to retreat. Anyone who turns his back on them, unless it is for a tactical advantage or to join another company, will incur Allah's wrath and Hell will be his home, truly a tortuous end. It was not you, but Allah, that killed them. It was not you whose blows destroyed them, but Allah destroyed them so that He might give the believers a gift from Himself. Allah is all-hearing and all-knowing. Therefore, Allah will certainly thwart the plans of the unbelievers.*

8:19 *Meccans! If you sought a judgment, it has now come to you. If you cease in your persecution of the believers, it will be better for you, but if you continue in your war against the faithful, so will We continue to help them. Your vast forces will be no match for Us for Allah stands with the faithful.*

1478 When Mohammed speaks, a Muslim has only one choice. Listen and obey.

8:20 *Believers! Be obedient to Allah and His messenger, and do not turn your backs now that you know the truth. Do not be like the ones who say, "We hear," but do not obey.*

1480 If those who practice the old religions will submit to Islam then all will be forgiven. Only submission to Islam will save the unbeliever.

8:38 *Tell the unbelievers that if they change their ways, then they would be forgiven for their past. If, however, they continue to sin, let them remember the fate of those who came before them. Fight against them until they stop persecuting you, and Allah's religion reigns sovereign over all others. If they cease, Allah knows all they do, but if they turn their backs, know that Allah is your protector—an excellent helper.*

60

1481 After war and victory there is the spoils of war. One fifth is to go to the Apostle, Allah's prophet.

> 8:41 *Know that a fifth of all your spoils of war [the traditional cut for the leader was a fourth] belong to Allah, to His messenger, to the messenger's family, the orphans, and needy travelers. Sincerely believe in Allah and in what was sent down to you through His messenger on the day of victory when the two armies met. Allah is powerful over all things.*

The Koran shows how Allah helped the Muslims destroy the unbelievers.

> 8:42 *Remember when you were camped on the near side of the valley and the unbelievers were on the far side with the caravan below you? If you had made an agreement to meet in battle [against the caravan], you surely would have failed, but you went into battle [against the unbelievers army], nevertheless, so that Allah could accomplish his goal that those who were destined to die would die and so those who were meant to live would live. Allah hears and knows all.*
>
> 8:43 *Allah showed your enemies to you in a dream as an army few in number. If He had shown you a large army, you certainly would have been frightened and you would have had arguments among yourselves. But Allah spared you this for He knows your deepest secrets. And when you met them in battle, He made them appear to you as fewer in number than in reality so that Allah might carry out what had to be done. All things return to Allah.*

1482 In war (jihad) remember Allah all the time and you will prevail. Obey Mohammed, don't argue with him or each other. Don't quit, don't lose morale. Allah will see that you prevail. And when the unbelievers are slain, their troubles have just begun. Allah will use his angels to torture them forever.

> 8:45 *Believers! When you confront their army stand fast and pray to Allah without ceasing so that you will be victorious. Obey Allah and His messenger, and do not argue with one another for fear that you will lose courage and strength. Be patient for Allah is with the patient. Do not be like the Meccans who left home bragging and full of vainglory. They prevent others from following Allah's path, but Allah knows all that they do.*
>
> 8:48 *Satan made their sinful acts seem acceptable to them, and he said, "No one will defeat you this day, and I will be there to help you." When the two armies came within sight of one another, however, he quickly fled saying, "I am finished with you for I can see things which you cannot [the angels were helping to kill the unbelievers]. I fear Allah for Allah's punishment is severe."*

I483-4 Mohammed is to encourage war and lead the believers to war. With Allah 20 Muslims can kill and vanquish 200 of the non-Muslims. And 100 Muslims can destroy 1000 of the non-Muslims. The unbelievers are ignorant and easily defeated by jihad. Take no prisoners until Islam has made all submit. Forget the ransom and the money, submission of the non-believers is all that matters.

> 8:65 *Messenger! Call the faithful to fight. If there are among you twenty who will stand fast, they will overcome two hundred; and if there are a hundred of you, they will overcome a thousand unbelievers for they lack understanding. Allah has now lessened your burden because He knows that there is weakness in you. If there are among you a hundred men who will stand fast, they will overcome two hundred; and if there are a thousand among you, they will, by the permission of Allah, overcome two thousand. Allah is with the steadfast.*
>
> 8:67 *A prophet should not take prisoners of war until he has fought and slaughtered in the land. You desire the bounty of the world, but Allah desires the bounty for you of the world to come. Allah is mighty and wise. If there had not been a prior command from Allah, you would have been punished severely for what you had taken. But now enjoy the spoils you have taken, which are lawful and good, but fear Allah. Allah is forgiving and merciful.*

THE RAID ON THE TRIBE OF B. SULAYM

I540-543, T1365 Seven days after Mohammed returned from Badr, there were four more armed raids, but no contact with the enemy, the unbelievers.

I484 Mohammed was now a political force unlike any ever seen in history. The fusion of religion and politics with a universal mandate created a historic force that is permanent. There will be no peace until all the world is Islam. The spoils of war will provide the wealth of Islam. The awe of Mohammed is the fear of Allah.

> B1,7,331 *The Prophet said, "I have been given five things which were not given to anyone else before me.*
>
> 1. *Allah made me victorious by awe, by His frightening my enemies for a distance of one month's journey.*
>
> 2. *The earth has been made for me and for my followers a place for praying and to perform my rituals, therefore anyone of my followers can pray wherever the time of a prayer is due.*
>
> 3. *The spoils of war has been made Halal (lawful) for me yet it was not lawful for anyone else before me.*

4. *I have been given the right of intercession on the Day of Resurrection.*

5. *Every Prophet used to be sent to his nation but only I have been sent to all mankind.*

Mohammed left Mecca as a preacher and prophet. He entered Medina with about 150 Muslim converts. After a year in Medina there were about 250-300 Muslims and most of them were very poor. After the battle of Badr, a new Islam emerged. Mohammed rode out of Medina as a politician and general. Islam became an armed political force with a religious motivation, jihad.

JIHAD AND THE KORAN

CHAPTER 11

*4:115 Anyone who opposes the Messenger after having
received Our guidance and follows a path other than
that of the true believer will be left to their own devices.
We will lead them into Hell, an evil home.*

- Jihad will continue until all unbelievers submit to Islam.
- Wounded or ailing jihadists should be supported by Islam.
- All Muslims should donate money for jihad.
- Jihadists strike terror into the hearts of unbelievers.
- No one can escape Islam.
- Jihadist can behead the unbelievers.
- Islam never offers peace while it is strong.
- Islam is relentless, it will never cease.

The Koran uses the term "fighting in Allah's cause" for jihad.

2:190 *And fight for Allah's cause [jihad] against those who fight you, but do not be the first to attack. Allah does not love the aggressors.*

2:191 *Kill them wherever you find them, and drive them out of whatever place from which they have driven you out for persecution [the Meccans made Mohammed leave] is worse than murder. But do not fight them inside the Holy Mosque unless they attack you there; if they do, then kill them. That is the reward for the unbelievers, but if they give up their ways, Allah is forgiving and merciful.*

2:193 *Fight them until you are no longer persecuted and the religion of Allah reigns absolute, but if they give up, then only fight the evil-doers. The defilement of a sacred month and sacred things are subject to the laws of retaliation. If anyone attacks you, attack him in the same way. Fear Allah and know that He is with those who believe.*

2:195 *Spend your wealth generously for Allah's cause [jihad] and do not use your own hands to contribute to your destruction. Do good, for surely Allah loves those that do good.*

Fight for Allah's Cause

2:244 *Fight for Allah's cause [jihad] and remember that He hears and knows everything.*

2:245 *Who will lend Allah a generous loan, which He will pay back multiple times? Allah gives generously and takes away, and you will return to Him.*

2:246 *Have you not considered what the leaders of the Children of Israel said to one of their messengers when Moses died? They said, "Appoint a king for us, and we will fight for the cause of Allah." He said, "What if you decline to fight when ordered to do so?" They said, "Why would we not fight for Allah when we and our children have been driven out of our homes?" But in the end, when they were ordered to fight all but a few refused. Allah knows the evil-doers.*

2:261 *Those who give their wealth for Allah's cause are like the grain of corn that grows seven ears with each ear having one hundred kernels. Allah will multiply the wealth of those He pleases. Allah is caring and all-knowing. Those who give their wealth for Allah's cause [jihad] and do not follow their gifts with guilt-inducing comments or insults will be rewarded by their Lord. They will have nothing about which to fear or grieve.*

2:273 *Charity is for those who have fought for Allah's cause and are now unable to work the land or travel to trade. The ignorant will think that they are wealthy because they are so modest, but you can tell them by their appearance. They do not beg people unrelentingly. Whatever charity you give will be known to Allah. Allah has placed His curse on usury and His blessing on charitable giving. Allah has no love for the ungrateful and sinful.*

Give Us Victory over the Unbelievers

2:286 *Allah does not give a soul more than it can withstand. It shall be rewarded for whatever good or evil it has done. Lord, do not punish us if we forget or make a mistake. Lord, do not give us a burden such as that which was given to those who came before us. Lord, do not give us more than we are able to withstand. Forgive us and forget our sins, and show us mercy. Only You are our protector, and give us victory over the unbelievers.*

Do Not Let the Unbelievers Think That They Will Escape Us

8:59 *Do not let the unbelievers think that they will escape Us. They have no power to escape. Gather against them all of your armed forces and cavalry so that you may strike terror into the hearts of the enemies of Allah and your enemy, and others besides them whom you do not know but whom Allah knows. All that you give for Allah's cause [jihad] will be repaid. You will be treated with fairness.*

8:61 *And if they are of a mind to make peace, then make peace too, and put your trust in Allah for He is all-hearing and all-knowing. But if they plan to betray you, surely Allah is sufficient for you. It is He who has strengthened you with His help and with the believers, giving them affection for one another. If you had given them all the earth's wealth, you could not have bound them together, but Allah has bound them, for He is mighty and wise. Oh messenger! Allah's strength is sufficient for you and your followers.*

They Have Already Betrayed Allah

8:70 *Messenger! Tell the captives who are under your control, "If Allah finds good in your hearts [if the prisoners convert to Islam], He will give you something better than that which has been taken away from you, and He will show you forgiveness. Truly, Allah is forgiving and merciful." If, however, they plot to betray you, know that they have already betrayed Allah. He has therefore given you power over them. Allah is all-knowing and wise.*

8:72 *Truly, those who believe and have left their homes and have given of their wealth and lives for Allah's cause, and those who have taken them in and helped them, will be as close as family to each other. But those who believed but did not leave their homes, you are not beholden to them until they also go into exile. But if they seek your help on account of the faith, it is your duty to help them except those against whom you have a treaty. Allah knows all that you do.*

8:73 *The unbelievers give comfort and protection to each other, therefore, if you do not do the same for one another, there will be oppression in the land and widespread corruption.*

8:74 *Those who have believed and have left their homes and fought for Allah's cause [jihad], and those who have taken them in and given them help, they are the true believers. They will receive mercy and generous provisions. Those who have believed and left their homes to fight with you since then, they are also a part of your family. According to Allah those who are related to you by blood are the closest to you. Allah knows all things.*

Cut off Their Heads

47:1 *Those who deny Allah and prevent others from following Allah's path, He will make their plans fail. Those who believe and do good works, however, and believe in what Mohammed has revealed, as it is the truth sent down from their Lord, He will cleanse them of their sins and improve their circumstances.*

47:3 *This is because the unbelievers follow lies while the believers follow the truth sent down from their Lord. It is in this manner that Allah sets forth the rules of conduct for mankind.*

47:4 *When you encounter the unbelievers on the battlefield, cut off their heads until you have thoroughly defeated them and then take the prisoners and tie them up firmly. Afterward, either allow them to go free or let them pay you their ransom until the war is over. This you are commanded. If it had been Allah's will he would have taken out His vengeance upon them, but He has commanded this so that He may test you by using these others. As for those who are killed for Allah's cause [jihad], He will not let their sacrifice be in vain. He will lead them into Paradise, of which He has told them.*

47:7 *Believers! If you help Allah's cause [jihad], Allah will help you and make you stand firm. But as for those who deny Allah, they will be destroyed. He will make their plans fail because they have rejected His revelations. He will thwart their tactics.*

Do Not Be Weak and Offer the Unbelievers Peace

47:33 *Believers! Obey Allah and the messenger, and do not let your effort be in vain. Those who do not believe and who prevent others from following Allah's path and then die as unbelievers will not receive Allah's forgiveness. Therefore, do not be weak and offer the unbelievers peace when you have the upper hand, for Allah is with you and will not begrudge you the reward of your deeds.*

47:34 *Those who do not believe and who prevent others from following Allah's path and then die as unbelievers will not receive Allah's forgiveness. Therefore, do not be weak and offer the unbelievers peace when you have the upper hand for Allah is with you and will not begrudge you the reward of your deeds.*

47:36 *Truly this present life is only for play and amusement, but if you believe and fear Him, He will give you your reward and will not ask you to give up your worldly wealth. But if He were to ask you for all of it and strongly urge you, you would become greedy, and this would reveal your hatred.*

47:38 *You are called upon to give to Allah's cause [jihad], but some of you are greedy. Whoever of you acts miserly does so only at the expense of his own soul. Truly, Allah has no use for you, but you have need for Him. If you turn your backs on Him, He will simply replace you with others who will not act like you!*

Stand Together in Battle Array like a Solid Wall

61:1 *All that is in the heavens and earth gives praise to Allah for He is mighty and wise.*

61:2 *Believers! Why do you say you do things that you never actually do? [At the battle of Uhud, some who had pledged courage fled and failed to fight.] It is most hateful in Allah's sight when you say one thing and yet do another.*

61:4 *Truly Allah loves those who fight for His cause and stand together in battle array like a solid wall.*

Fight Valiantly for Allah's Cause

61:10 *Believers! Should I show you a profitable exchange that will keep you from severe torment? Believe in Allah and His messenger and fight valiantly for Allah's cause [jihad] with both your wealth and your lives. It would be better for you, if you only knew it!*

61:12 *He will forgive you of your sins and lead you into Gardens beneath which rivers flow. He will keep you in beautiful mansions in the Gardens of Eden. That is the ultimate triumph. And He will give you other blessings for which you long: help from Allah and a swift victory. Give the good news to the believers.*

61:14 *Believers! Be Allah's helpers just as Jesus, son of Mary, said to his disciples, "Who will help me to do the work of Allah?" and they replied, "We are Allah's helpers." Some among the Children of Israel believed in him and others did not. But for those who believed, We gave them victory over their enemies.*

57:10 *And for what reason should you not give to Allah's cause [jihad], when the heavens and earth are Allah's inheritance alone? Those of you who gave to the cause before the victory and fought will receive a greater reward than those who gave and fought after it. But Allah has promised a good reward to all of you. Allah knows all that you do. Who will loan generously to Allah? He will pay him back double what he is owed, and he will receive a noble reward.*

Seize Them and Kill Them Wherever They Are

4:91 *You will also find others who seek to gain your confidence as well as that of their own people. Every time they are thrown back into temptation, they fall into it deeply. If they do not keep away from you or offer you peace or withdraw their hostilities, then seize them and kill them wherever they are. We give you complete authority over them.*

When You Travel Abroad to Fight for Allah's Cause

4:94 *Believers! When you travel abroad to fight for Allah's cause [jihad], be discerning, and do not say to everyone who greets you, "You are not a believer," only seeking the fleeting joys of this world [by killing the unbeliever and taking their property]. With Allah are abundant joys. You too were like them before Allah granted His grace to you. Therefore, be perceptive; Allah knows all that you do.*

4:95 *Believers who stay at home in safety, other than those who are disabled, are not equal to those who fight with their wealth and their lives for Allah's cause [jihad]. Allah has ranked those who fight earnestly with their wealth and lives above those who stay at home. Allah has promised good things to all, but those who fight for Him will receive a far greater reward than those who have not. They will be conferred ranks especially from Him, along with forgiveness and mercy, for Allah is forgiving and merciful.*

Do Not Relent in Pursuing the Enemy

4:100 *Those who leave their homes for Allah's cause [jihad] will find many places of refuge and provisions in the earth. Those who leave their homes flying to fight for Allah and His Messenger and die, their reward from Allah is assured. Allah is gracious and merciful!*

4:101 *When you go forth through the land for war, you will not be blamed if you cut your prayers short because you fear that the unbelievers are about to attack you for the unbelievers are your undoubted enemies.*

4:102 *And when you [Mohammed] are with the believers conducting prayer, let a group of them stand up with you, taking their weapons with them. After they have prostrated themselves, let them go back to the rear and allow another group to come up and pray with you, also allowing them to be armed. It would please the unbelievers if you failed to carry your weapons and luggage so that they could attack you all at once. You will not be blamed if you lay down your weapons when a heavy rain impedes you or when you are sick, but you must always be vigilant. Allah has prepared a disgraceful torment for the unbelievers.*

4:103 *And when you have finished your prayers, remember Allah when you are standing, sitting, and lying down. But when you are free from danger, attend to your prayers regularly for prayer at certain times is commanded for believers.*

4:104 *Do not relent in pursuing the enemy. If you are suffering, so are they, but you have hope from Allah while they have none. Allah is all-knowing and wise!*

22:58 *Those who fled their homes for Allah's cause [jihad] and were killed or died as a result, surely Allah will provide for them generously, for Allah is the best provider. Allah will certainly lead them in with a pleasing welcome. Allah is all-knowing and gracious. So it will be. Whoever retaliates with the same force with which he was wronged and continues to be oppressed, Allah will help him. Allah is merciful and forgiving.*

Fight Valiantly for Allah's Cause

22:78 *Fight valiantly for Allah's cause [jihad] as it benefits you to do for Him. He has chosen you, and has not made hardships for you in the religion; it is the religion of your father Abraham. It was Allah who called you Muslims, both in previous scriptures and now, so that the Messenger may be a witness for you and that you may be his witness against mankind. Therefore, pray regularly, pay the poor tax, and hold firmly to Allah, for He is your protector. He is he best protector and the best helper.*

So Make War on Them

9:8 *How can there be a treaty for the others, since if they prevailed against you, they would not respect your agreement? They will speak fair words from their mouths, but their hearts will be against you. Most of them are rebellious and wicked. They have made some gains with the signs of Allah, and they have hindered many from His way. Evil is what they do. They do not respect the ties of blood or faith regarding the believers. These are the wrongdoers. Yet if they turn to Allah, observe regular prayer, and practice regular charity, they are your brothers in religion. We explain Our signs in detail for those who understand.*

9:12 *If the unbelievers break their oaths and revile your religion after an alliance is made, then fight the leaders of unbelief, for their oaths are nothing to them, so they may be stopped. Will you not fight against those Meccans who have broken their oaths, plotted to expel your Messenger, and attacked you first? Do you fear them? Allah is more worthy of your fear, if you are believers. So make war on them. Allah will punish them by your hands. He will put them to shame and will give you victory over them. He will heal the hearts of the believers and will remove the wrath in their hearts. Allah gives mercy to whom He will. Allah is knowing and wise.*

9:16 *Do you think that you will be abandoned as if Allah did not yet know those among you who struggle and who have not taken anyone for friends beside Allah, His apostle, and the faithful? Allah is well aware of what you do.*

5:33 *The only reward for those who war against Allah and His messengers and strive to commit mischief on the earth is that they will be slain or crucified, have their alternate hands and feet cut off, or be banished from the land. This will be their disgrace in this world, and a great torment shall be theirs in the next except those who repent before you overpower them. Know that Allah is forgiving and merciful.*

5:35 *Oh you who believe, fear Allah, and seek the means to be near Him. Strive earnestly on his path so that you may attain happiness.*

How Could You Not Fight for Allah's Cause?

4:69 *Those who obey Allah and His Messenger will live with the messengers and the saints and the martyrs and the righteous. What wonderful company! This is the bounty of Allah, and Allah's infinite knowledge is sufficient. Believers! Be cautious, and either march forward in groups or advance all together. There are some among you who are sure to hang back, and if a disaster came upon you, would say, "Allah has dealt with us graciously because we were not in the battle." If, however, you were met with victory, they, as if there were no friendship between you, would*

70

say, "If only I had been with them! Surely I would have been greatly successful!"

4:74 *Let those who would sell the life of this world for the world to come fight for Allah's cause [jihad]. Whoever fights for Allah's cause, whether he is killed or is victorious, We will grant him a great reward. How could you not fight for Allah's cause? For the weak men, women, and children who plead, "Lord! Rescue us from this city of oppressors [Mecca]. Send us a protector from Your presence; send a defender from Your presence."*

4:76 *The believers fight for Allah's cause [jihad] and the unbelievers fight for Satan. Therefore, fight against the friends of Satan. Truly Satan's strategy is weak.*

4:77 *Look at those who were told, "Lay down your arms of war for a time, attend to your prayers, and pay the poor tax." When they were told to resume fighting, some of them feared their fellow man more than they should have feared Allah, and said, "Lord! Why have you commanded us to fight? Why could you not have given us a longer respite?" Say: The joys of this world are fleeting. The world to come will be better for those of you who fear Allah, and you will never be treated unfairly in the least. Wherever you are, death will find you, even if you lock yourselves in high towers! If something good happens to them they say, "This is from Allah," but if something evil happens to them they say, "It was the Messenger's fault." Say: Everything is from Allah! But what is wrong with these people that they fail to understand what is told to them?*

Oh, Messenger, Make War on the Unbelievers and Hypocrites

66:9 *Oh, Messenger, make war on the unbelievers and hypocrites, and be hard on them. Hell will be their home, and wretched is the passage to it.*

66:10 *Allah sets forth as an example to unbelievers the wife of Noah and the wife of Lot. They were under two of Our righteous servants yet they both deceived them, so their husbands did not help them at all against Allah. It was said to them, "Enter into the Fire with those who enter."*

66:11 *Allah also holds forth to those who believe the example of the wife of Pharaoh. She said, "Lord, build me a house with you in Paradise and deliver me from Pharaoh and his doings and deliver me from the wicked."*

66:12 *Mary, the daughter of Imran who guarded her chastity and into whose womb We breathed of Our spirit, accepted the words of her Lord and of His revelations. She was one of the obedient.*

JIHAD, THE JEWS' EXILE

CHAPTER 12

*61:11 Believe in Allah and His messenger and fight valiantly
for Allah's cause [jihad] with both your wealth and your
lives. It would be better for you, if you only knew it!*

- Whole ethnic groups can be driven from Islamic areas.
- Jews are unique enemies of Islam.
- The wealth of non-Muslims can be taken by force and threats.
- Intellectuals, artists, and political commentators can be killed for resisting Islam.
- Killing a few members of a community will allow Islam to terrorize and control the rest.
- Violence attracts people to Islam.
- Lies and deceit that advance Islam are skillful actions of jihad.

Mohammed now challenged the first of the three Jewish tribes. They refused his offer of Islam. Soon he attacked the first Jewish tribe and won. Mohammed took all of their wealth and exiled them.

Mohammed continued his profitable jihad against the Meccan caravans.

Mohammed ordered his first assassination against a Jew who wrote poems against him. He then ordered the assassination of other Jews.

THE AFFAIR OF THE JEWS OF QAYNUQA

I545 There were three tribes of Jews in Medina. The Beni Qaynuqa were gold smiths and lived in a stronghold in their quarters. It is said by Mohammed that they broke the treaty that had been signed when Mohammed came to Medina. How they did this is unclear.

I545 Mohammed assembled the Jews in their market and said: "Oh Jews, be careful that Allah does not bring vengeance upon you like what happened to the Quraysh. Become Muslims. You know that I am the prophet that was sent you. You will find that in your scriptures."

I545 They replied: "Oh Mohammed you seem to think that we are your people. Don't fool yourself. You may have killed and beaten a few merchants of the Quraysh, but we are men of war and real men."

I546 Some time later Mohammed besieged the Jews in the their quarters. None of the other two Jewish tribes came to their support. Finally the Jews surrendered and expected to be slaughtered after their capture.

I546 But an Arab ally bound to them by a client relationship approached Mohammed and said, "Oh Mohammed deal kindly with my clients." Mohammed ignored him. The ally repeated the request and again Mohammed ignored him. The ally grabbed Mohammed by the robe and enraged Mohammed who said, "Let me go!" The ally said, "No, you must deal kindly with my clients. They have protected me and now you would kill them all? I fear these changes." The response by the Koran:

> 5:51 *Oh, believers, do not take the Jews or Christians as friends. They are but one another's friends. If any one of you take them for his friends, he surely is one of them. Allah will not guide the evildoers.*
> 5:52 *You will see those who have a diseased heart race towards them and say, "We fear in case a change of fortune befalls us." Perhaps Allah will bring about some victory or event of His own order. Then they will repent of the thoughts they secretly held in their hearts.*

Mohammed exiled the Jews and took all of their wealth and goods.

THE RAID TO AL QARADA

I547 Mohammed's victory at Badr and ongoing jihad caused the Quraysh to go a different route to Syria. They hired a new guide to take them over the new route. Mohammed had intelligence about their route and sent a party to raid them. They were carrying a great deal of silver when the caravan stopped at a watering hole. The Muslims surprised them and the Quraysh managed to escape but Mohammed's men were able to steal all the caravan's goods, including the silver. The stolen goods were delivered to Mohammed in Medina.

THE ASSASSINATION OF AL ASHRAF, THE JEW

I548 When Al Ashraf, a Jew of Medina, heard that two of his friends had been killed at Badr, he said that the grave was a better place than the earth with Mohammed. So the "enemy of Allah" composed some poems bewailing the loss of his friends and attacking Islam.

I551 When Mohammed heard of Al Ashraf's criticism of his politics, he said, "Who will rid me of Al Ashraf?" A Muslim said, "I will kill him for you." Days later Mohammed found out that his assassin was not doing anything, including eating or drinking. Mohammed summoned him and asked what was going on. The man replied that he had taken on a task that was too difficult for him to do. Mohammed said that it was a duty which he should try to do. The assassin said, "Oh Apostle of Allah, I will have to tell a lie." The Prophet said, "Say what you like, you are free in the matter."

I552 By the use of lies three Muslims were able to kill Al Ashraf. When they returned to Mohammed, he was praying. They told him that they had killed the enemy of Allah. Their attack terrorized all the Jews. There was no Jew in Medina who was not afraid.

KILL ANY JEW THAT FALLS INTO YOUR POWER

I554 The Apostle of Allah said, "Kill any Jew who falls into your power." Hearing this Muhayyisa fell upon a Jewish merchant who was a business associate and killed him. His brother was not a Muslim and asked him how he could kill a man who had been his friend and partner in many business deals. The Muslim said that if Mohammed had asked him to kill his brother he would have done it immediately. His brother said, "You mean that if Mohammed said to cut off my head you would do it?" "Yes," was the reply. The older brother then said, "By Allah, any religion which brings you to this is marvelous." And he decided then and there to become a Muslim.

JIHAD, A SETBACK

CHAPTER 13

*4:14 But those who disobey Allah and His Messenger
and go beyond His limits, will be led into the Fire to
live forever, and it will be a humiliating torment!*

- Islam's enemies will not try to destroy Islam, but will try to induce reason in Islam and be fair. Nonbelievers do not recognize the threat of annihilation by jihad.
- A jihadist does not become discouraged when suffering a failure.
- A jihadist obeys his leader.
- Success comes from following the way of Allah.
- Assassination of those who resist Islam is a constant of jihad.
- Artists and intellectuals who speak against Islam may be threatened and assassinated.

The Meccans came to Medina with an army to seek revenge against their declared enemy, Mohammed. He decided to leave the security of the Medinan walls and meet in the field of battle.

At first the Muslims prevailed, but their greed about the spoils caused them to break ranks and lose the advantage to the Medinans. But the Medinans did not try to crush Islam. After they had killed about as many Muslims as they had lost (the old tribal warfare rules), they retired.

It was a big loss for Mohammed as he also lost his best warrior, Hamza. But the battle was important for Islam. It showed that Muslims must never vary from Mohammed's orders. Allah may be on the side of Islam, but Muslims must never falter. Of course, all of the slain Muslims warriors went to Paradise.

There would be more battles. Muslims must learn from their losses. Mohammed sent our assassins against one of his enemies and an artist.

THE BATTLE OF UHUD

1555 Back at Mecca those who had lost at the battle of Badr told others, "Men of Quraysh, Mohammed has killed your best men. Give us money so that we may take revenge." Money was raised, men were hired. An army was put together.

1558 So the Meccans camped near Medina, ready for war. Ready for revenge. The Muslims now needed a strategy. Many, including Mohammed, wanted to sit and let the Meccans attack Medina. The town itself could be used in a defensive way—walls and rooftops would give any defender a strong advantage. But blood ran hot with the Muslim warriors. They were not afraid to meet the Meccans on the field of combat, man to man. After Badr, they were invincible. Allah had said as much. They said, "Mohammed lead us to our enemies, don't let them think that we are weak and cowards." The arguments went on until Mohammed went in his house and came out in his armor.

1559 But now, seeing him in his armor, the hot bloods repented and said that they should never try to persuade Mohammed to do anything. They had been wrong. Mohammed said, "When a prophet puts on his armor, he should not take it off until there has been war." So he marched out with a 1000 men to meet the Meccans.

1560 When they saw the Meccans, Mohammed said, "Let there be no fighting until I give the word." What they saw made the Muslims' blood boil. The Meccans had put their camels and horses into the crops of the Muslims. Mohammed placed 50 archers to protect his rear and flank. They must not move but hold that ground. Mohammed put on a second coat of mail (armor).

1562 The morrow came and the battle was to begin. Now the Meccans had brought their women for the sole purpose to urge on the men. Men do not want to be cowards in front of women. The women began to beat their tambourines and chant poetry:

If you advance we will hug you
And place soft rugs beneath you
If you retreat we will leave you
Leave and no more love you.

1570 The Muslims fought without fear and the battle went against the Meccans who were cut off from their camp that had the spoils of war. The Muslim archers left their positions to get to the spoils. The battle might go to Islam, but the treasure would be theirs. This left the flank and rear open and the Meccan cavalry took advantage and charged the rear where Mohammed was. The battle suddenly went against the Muslims.

1571 The Muslims were put to flight and many were slain. Even Mohammed got hit in the face by a rock, broke a tooth and split his lip. He was incensed. The Meccans were all around and the Muslims had to protect him with their bodies.

1574 At one point the Meccans thought that they had killed the man who had brought them so much pain. But one Muslim recognized the prophet under his helmet and spread the news of his living. Mohammed fled the field. He was a heavy man, and wore two suits of armor. He almost could not climb the rocks and hill without help.

1583 The day went to the Meccans, the Quraysh. The Meccans did not press their advantage. They came to extract tribal justice and they killed about as many the Muslims had killed at Badr. They did not want to dominate Islam. Abu Sufyan, the Meccan leader, agreed through an emissary that they would meet in combat next year.

> We have paid you back for Badr
> And a war that follows a war is violent
> I could not bear the loss of my friends
> Nor my brother and his uncle and my first born.
> I have slaked my vengeance and fulfilled my vow.
> The slave who killed Hamza has cooled the burning in my breast
> I shall thank the slave now free
> Until my bones rot in the grave.   —Hind

1586 The dead Muslims were buried in the battlefield. Mohammed said, "I testify that none who are wounded in jihad but what he will be raised by Allah with his bleeding wounds smelling like the finest perfume." When Mohammed heard the women weeping for their dead, but he wanted wailing for his uncle Hamza as well. So the women wailed for Hamza and Mohammed felt better.

1587 When Mohammed entered his house he handed his sword to his daughter and told her, "Wash the blood from this for by Allah it has served me well today." The next day he ordered all the fighters who had been at Uhud to marshal themselves and be ready to head out to pursue the enemy. This move was pure strategy to impress the enemy that he was still strong and not weakened by his losses. They went about eight miles from Medina and camped for three days before returning to Medina.

1589 Mohammed was the supreme master of the psychology of war. He sent an agent, who pretended to be a friend of the Meccans, to Abu Sufyan, the Meccan leader. Abu Sufyan was thinking about going back and finishing off the Muslims. But Mohammed's agent told Abu Sufyan that Mohammed was coming very soon with an army, the like of which had never been seen. They were in a state of total fury and would sweep into Hell all that were in front of them. Abu Sufyan, the merchant, left for Mecca and security. They had settled their score.

THE KORAN AND THE BATTLE OF UHUD

Since Allah had sent angels to the previous battle of Badr and the out-numbered Muslims triumphed, how could they fail at Uhud?

1593 Two of the clans of Muslims had doubts about the battle. But Allah was their friend and they did not doubt Islam and went on into the battle because of their belief in Allah and Mohammed.

> 3:121 *Remember when you [Mohammed] left your home early in the morning to lead the believers to their battle stations [battle of Uhud]? Allah heard and knew all. When two of your brigades showed cowardice, Allah protected them both. Let the faithful put their trust in Allah. Allah made you victorious at Badr when you were the weaker army. Therefore, fear Allah and be grateful to Him. Then you said to the believers, "Is it not enough for you that your Lord helped you by sending down three thousand angels?" Yes! And if you stand firm and fear Allah and you are suddenly attacked by your enemies, Allah will send down five thousand angels to wreak havoc upon them.*

1595 The reason for the loss was that the archers did not hold their ground, When they saw that the Meccans were cut off from their camp, they ran to get the spoils of war. Greed caused them to disobey Mohammed. So they should always obey Mohammed, he speaks for the Lord of all. Those who did not follow orders should ask for forgiveness. If they will see that it was their fault and be remorseful they can still get their reward of heaven.

1597 The reason that Allah let the Meccans win was to test the Muslims. Now they will know their true selves. Are they fair weather friends of Mohammed or can they see their faults? If they obey Mohammed, then they can become true Muslims. A true Muslim never loses his morale, never falls into despair.

1596 If you have been wounded or suffered losses in the battle, don't forget that the non-Muslims have also suffered. Over the long view, fortunes go up and down. You must take the long view and believe in Mohammed and know that all will turn out well in the end. But those who died have the best reward. They are martyrs for Islam. Those who do wrong are the hypocrites, the pretenders.

3:140 If you have been wounded [Muslims lost the battle of Uhud], be certain that the same has already befallen your enemies. We bring misfortune to mankind in turns so that Allah can discern who are the true believers, and so that We may select martyrs from among you. Allah does not love those who do evil. It is also Allah's purpose to test the believers and to destroy the unbelievers.

1596 The Muslims must realize that Allah will purify them through tests such as the one they have just had. Those of true faith will not be discouraged. The hypocrites will be exposed and deprived of all blessing. Do you think you will get to heaven before Allah has tested you? Allah must know who is really a believer. A Muslim warrior must be given a trial. Losing at Uhud is merely a trial. After the big victory at Badr, those who were not there wanted to be part of the winning army. They were anxious to be able to show off as warriors, but when the actual killing started, many were not as good as they thought they would be.

3:142 Did you think that you would be permitted into Paradise before Allah tested you to see who would fight for His cause [jihad] and endure until the end? You used to wish for death before you saw it, but now that you have seen it with your own eyes, you turn and run from it. Mohammed is only a messenger, and many messengers have come before him. If he died or was killed, would you turn your backs on the faith? But those who do in fact turn their backs will not hurt Allah in the least. And Allah will surely reward those who serve Him with gratitude.

1597 The Muslims should not think that they are the first to experience failure. In history many have failed in jihad, but they never lost heart or weakened. The lesson of Uhud is to be firm and not get depressed over a small failure.

3:146 Many of the messengers have fought for Allah's cause [jihad] alongside large armies. They were never frightened by what they encountered on Allah's path, nor did they weaken or cringe with fear. Allah loves those who stand firm. Their only cry was this, "Lord! Forgive us of our sins and the things we have done that were against our duty; help us stand firm and make us victorious over the unbelievers." Therefore, Allah gave them their reward in this world, as well as an excellent reward in the world to come. Allah loves those who do good.

1599 Do not think that the jihad is over. Soon Islam will bring terror to the unbelievers. After death, they will burn in Hell. The evil that will bring about their destruction is that they do not practice the religion of Islam.

3:149 *Believers! If you follow the unbelievers, they will cause you to reject the faith and lead you to eternal damnation. But Allah is your protector and the best of helpers. We will strike terror into the hearts of the unbelievers because they worship others besides Allah, which He gave them no permission to do. Their home will be the Fire, a terrible resting place for the evil-doers.*

1599 Your slaughter of the unbelievers went well and you were about to wipe the unbelievers off the face of the earth, thanks to Allah. But then you disobeyed Mohammed. Allah did not destroy you because he is merciful. But your greed is of this world and you wanted the spoils of war of this world. But you must desire what comes after death, not the wealth of this world. You must learn this lesson with the grace of Allah.

3:152 *Allah fulfilled His covenant with you [Mohammed] when He allowed you to destroy your enemies [at the battle of Badr]. And then later, when you [the Muslims at Uhud] lost your courage, arguments broke out among you [the Muslims disobeyed orders and broke ranks to run and get the exposed spoils of the Meccans] and you sinned after you had come so close to what you wanted [spoils of war]. Some of you wish for the desires of this world and some of you for the world to come. Therefore, He caused you to be defeated so that you might be tested. Now He has forgiven you for Allah shows grace to the believers.*
3:153 *Remember when you [at Uhud the Muslims broke and fled] ran up the hill in cowardice and paid no attention to anyone and the messenger was behind you calling you back to the battle? Allah rewarded you with trouble for the trouble you caused Him so that you would not grieve for the spoils you lost or for what happened to you. Allah knows all that you do.*

1601 After the battle some were at ease, but others were in a state of anxiety because they did not trust Allah. The hypocrites divorced themselves from the decision and blamed others for failure. If they had had their way then everyone would have been safe. But when Allah decrees your time has come, nothing can stay the hand of death. Death must come and it is better to die in jihad.

Those who die in jihad will be rewarded by Allah.

3:157 *The forgiveness and mercy they, who die or are killed for Allah's cause, will receive from Allah will be far better than anything they could have gained. If you die or are killed, then surely you will all be gathered before Allah.*

1602 But Mohammed must be gentle with the Muslims. So he will over-look their faults and will forgive them. He will still consult with them, but the final decision must lie with Allah and Mohammed.

> 3:158 *It was because of Allah's mercy that you spoke so gently to them. For if you had dealt with them severely or been hard-hearted, they would have turned away from you. Therefore, forgive them and ask Allah to forgive them and counsel them in the affair of war; and when you have resolved the matters, put your trust in Allah. Allah loves those who trust Him. If Allah is helping you, no one can defeat you. But if He leaves you, who will be there to help you when He is gone? Therefore, let the faithful put their trust in Allah.*

1603 The Muslim's loss was a test that was brought on by their decisions. The hypocrites were told to fight in jihad or at least defend the city. Their excuses are those of an unbeliever.

> 3:165 *And when disaster [battle of Uhud] befell you, although it brought destruction twice as great to the unbelievers, you said, "Why is this hap-pening to us?" Say to them, "You have brought this upon yourselves for Allah controls all things. The destruction which befell you the day the two armies met in battle was Allah's will so He would recognize who were the true believers and who were the hypocrites." And when they were told, "Come and fight for Allah's cause [jihad] and drive your en-emies back," they replied, "If we knew how to fight, then we would have followed you."*
> 3:168 *Some of them were closer to unbelief than faith that day. What they said with their mouths was not what was in their hearts, but Allah knew what they were hiding in their hearts. It was these who said, while sitting at home, of their brothers, "If only they had listened to us, then they would not have been killed." Say: Try to avert your death if what you say is true!*
> 3:169 *Never believe that those who have been killed for Allah's cause [jihad] are dead. No, they are alive with their Lord and receive rich pro-visions. They rejoice in the bounty Allah gives them and are joyful for those left behind who have yet to join them that they will have nothing fear or regret. They are filled with joy for Allah's grace and blessings. Al-lah will not fail to reward the faithful.*

1606 The success that the unbelievers are experiencing is temporary. They will grow in their evil and they will be punished. Allah will not leave the believers in this state. But this trial will separate the weak from the strong.

ASSASSINATION AS JIHAD

M276 After Uhud, several tribes allied themselves under the leadership of Sufyan Ibn Khalid. Mohammed dispatched an assassin to kill him, for without his leadership the coalition would fall apart. So the assassin, Abdullah, joined his forces and waited until he was alone with him. He killed Sufyan and cut off his head and went back to Medina.

M276 Abdullah then went straight to Mohammed. Mohammed welcomed him and asked him how it went. Abdullah presented Mohammed with the head of his enemy. Mohammed was gratified and presented him with his walking stick. He said, "This is a token between you and me on the day of resurrection. Very few will have such to lean on in that day." Abdullah attached it to his sword scabbard.

THE RAID ON THE MUSTALIQ TRIBE

1725 When Mohammed heard that the Arab tribe, the Mustaliq, were opposed to him and were gathering against him, he set out with his army to attack them. He contacted them at a watering hole and combat started. Islam was victorious and the Mustaliq and their women, children, and goods were taken as spoils of war and distributed to the fighters.

1729 The captives of the tribe of Mustaliq were parceled out as spoils. There was a ransom price set upon their heads. If the ransom were not paid then the people were treated as spoils and slaves. Now one of them was a beautiful woman with a high price on her. She came to Mohammed and asked him to see if the price could be reduced. Mohammed had a better idea. He would pay the ransom for the beautiful woman and she would become his wife. Now in spite of the fact that she was already married, there was no problem. It was a deal. Mohammed paid the ransom and the beautiful woman became wife number seven.

1729 This marriage had a side effect. The captives were now related to Mohammed's wife. They were all released without ransom.

THE DEATH OF A POETESS

1996 There was a poetess who wrote a poem against Islam. Mohammed said, "Who will rid me of Marwan's daughter?" One of his followers heard him and on that very night he went to the woman's home to kill her.

M239 The assassin was able to do the work in the dark as the woman slept. Her other children lay in the room, but her babe lay on her breast.

The stealthy assassin removed the child and drove the knife into her with such force that he pined her to the bed.

1996 In the morning he went to Mohammed and told him. Mohammed said, "You have helped Allah and his Apostle." When asked about the consequences, Mohammed said, "Two goats won't butt their heads together over this."

M239 Mohammed turned to the people in the mosque, he said, "If you wish to see a man who has assisted Allah and his Prophet, look here." Omar cried, "What, the blind Omeir!" "No," said Mohammed, "call him Omeir the Seeing."

1996 The poetess had five sons and the assassin went to them and said, "I killed Bint Marwan, Oh sons. Withstand me if you can; don't keep me waiting." Islam became powerful that day and many became Muslims when they saw the power of Islam.

JIHAD, THE JEWS SUBMIT

CHAPTER 14

58:20 Those who oppose Allah and His Messenger will be laid low. Allah has declared, "Surely I will be victorious, along with My messengers." Truly Allah is strong and mighty.

- Non-Muslims do not work together against Islam.
- Jihad attacks economic targets.
- The wealth of non-Muslims can be taken by force.
- The act of an individual against Islam may bring destruction to his entire community and family.
- Spies are a part of jihad.
- Islam adopts new methods of war from non-Muslims.
- Islam sows discord among its enemies.

Mohammed now attacked the second of the three Jewish tribes that had been in Medina. They were date farmers and he burned their plantations. They surrendered and Mohammed took all of their wealth and drove them from Medina.

The Meccans returned with an army to attack Mohammed. But he installed a trench (a unique strategy in Arabia) and foiled the Meccan plans. Mohammed used both spies and secret agents to work behind the scenes and weaken the Meccan alliances.

CLEANSING

I652 It had been four years since Mohammed came to Medina. Mohammed went to one of the two remaining Jewish tribes to ask for blood money for the two men his fighter had killed. At first they said yes, but as they talked about it they decided that this would be a good time to kill Mohammed. Here he was in their quarter of Medina sitting on a wall near a roof. Why not send a man up and drop a rock on this man who had been such a sorrow to them? Mohammed got word of the plot and left.

84

I653 This was as good a reason as any to deal with the Jews. The same Jews who insisted that he was not the prophet. He raised his army and went off to put their fortresses under siege. These Jews were farmers and they grew the finest dates in all of Arabia. So Mohammed cut and burned their date palms as they watched. They called out, "You have prohibited wanton destruction and blamed those who do that. Now you do what you forbid."

I653 Now the other Jewish tribe had assured them that they would come to their defense. But no Jew would stand with another Jew against Islam. With no help from their brothers, the besieged Jews cut a deal with the apostle of Allah. Spare their lives and let them go with what they could carry on their camels, except for their armor.

I654 When there was fighting in jihad, the fighter got four-fifths. But since there had been no fighting there was no reason to give four-fifths to the jihadists. All of the spoils went to Mohammed, not just one fifth.

I654 There were some new problems created—the burning of the date palms and all the money going to Mohammed. The Koran had the answers. It was Allah who wrecked his vengeance upon the Jews and gave Mohammed power over them. It was even Allah who caused the Jews to tear down their own houses.

> 59:2 *It was He who caused the People of the Book [the Jews] to leave their homes and go into the first exile. They did not think they would leave, and they thought that their fortresses could protect them from Allah. But Allah's wrath reached them from where they did not expect it and cast terror into their hearts, so that they destroyed their homes with their own hands, as well as by the hands of the believers. Take warning from this example, you who have the eyes to see it!*

I654 And the Jews were very fortunate that Allah let them go with a few worldly possessions. They got out alive, Allah did not slay them, but they will burn in Hell since they resisted Mohammed. Resist Islam and Allah will punish you. As far as the wanton destruction of the palm trees, that cannot be laid to Mohammed, it was the Jew's fault. They should have done what Allah wanted and then the Jews would not have suffered Allah's vengeance.

> 59:3 *And if Allah had not decreed their exile, surely He would have punished them in this world. And in the world to come they will receive the punishment of the Fire because they had disobeyed Allah and His Messenger. Whoever disobeys Allah, knows that Allah is truly severe in His punishment.*

> 59:5 *Allah gave you permission to cut down some palm trees and leave others intact so as to shame the wicked [the Jews]. After Allah gave the spoils to His Messenger, you made no move with horses or camels to capture them [the Jews], but Allah gives His messengers power over what He chooses. Allah is all-powerful.*

1654 As for all the spoils of war going to Mohammed, there was no actual fighting, hence no need to give spoils to fighters. Mohammed can do as he wishes.

> 59:7 *The spoils of war taken from the people in the cities and given by Allah to His Messenger belong to Allah, to His Messenger and to his family, to the orphans, to the poor, and to the wayfaring traveler so that it will not stay among those of you who are wealthy. Take what the Messenger has offered you, and refuse what he has forbidden you. And fear Allah, for Allah is severe in His punishment.*
> 59:8 *A part of the spoils of war also belong to the poor refugees: the Immigrants driven from their homes and possessions who seek Allah's grace and help Allah and His Messenger. These are the sincere believers.*

THE BATTLE OF THE TRENCH

1669 Some of the Jews who had been exiled from Medina decided that they needed to destroy Mohammed and to do that they needed allies. Since allies were to be found in Mecca, they went there and parlayed with the leaders of the Quraysh. But since this was a war of religion, the Quraysh wanted was proof of religious supremacy to Mohammed. So the leaders said to the Jews, "You are People of the Book and you know our disagreement. Who has the better religion, us or Mohammed?" The leaders of the Jews replied that the Quraysh had the better religion.

1669 Now the Koran could not pass up such an insult to Mohammed. So the Koran says:

> 4:49 *Have you not seen those who praise themselves for their purity? But Allah purifies whom He pleases, and they will not be treated unjustly in the slightest degree. See how they make up lies about Allah! That in itself is a terrible sin. Have you not seen those [Jews allied with the Meccans] to whom part of the Scriptures were given? They believe in idols and sorcery, and they say of the unbelievers, "These are guided on a better path than the believers." It is on these whom Allah has laid His curse. Those who are cursed by Allah will have no one to help them.*

1669-670 So the Meccans entered into an alliance with the Jews. Another Arab tribe joined the alliance as well.

As Mohammed had many spies in Mecca, so it took no time until he knew of the coming fight and he set out to prepare for it. There was a Persian who suggested to Mohammed that he build a trench as a barrier against the Meccans and their allies. For eight days the Arabs worked at building a trench, or ditch, around the weak points of Medina. To help with morale Mohammed personally pitched in and did his turn at manual labor.

I671 There was a fair amount of slacking and leaving work. The labor problems even worked their way into the Koran:

> 24:62 *Only those who believe in Allah and His Messenger are the true believers, and when they are gathered together, do not leave until they have sought his permission. Those who ask your permission are the ones who truly believe in Allah and His Messenger. And when they ask your permission to leave for personal reasons, give permission to whom you please, and ask Allah for His indulgence on their behalf, for Allah is indulgent, merciful.*

I673 But the work was done just in time. The Quraysh and the other allies camped near the trench. Mohammed and his army camped on their side of the trench and sent the women and children to the forts.

I674 One of the exiled Jews approached the last tribe of Jews in Medina to be allies with the attacking Meccans. At first the Jews would not even talk to him. After all, if Mohammed won, they would be left with the consequences of dealing with a man who had driven the other two tribes of Jews from Medina. But in the end the Jews agreed to lend aid if the battle started to go against Mohammed.

I677-683 Mohammed was able to use his agents to sow discord among those allied against him. The trench defense frustrated the Meccans. The weather was bad and the allies were distrustful of each other. In terms of actual combat only a handful of men were killed over the twenty-day siege. The Meccans broke camp and went back home. It was a victory for Mohammed.

> 33:9 *Believers! Remember Allah's grace when your enemies attacked you [the Battle of the Ditch], and We set a mighty wind against them [the Meccans and their allies, the confederates, put Medina under siege], and warriors they could not see, but Allah sees clearly all that you do. [The confederates' poor planning, poor leadership, and bad weather caused them to fail]*

JIHAD, THE JEWS AGAIN

CHAPTER 15

*58:5 Those who oppose Allah and His Messenger will
be laid low, just as those who came before them.*

• Jihad will not cease until every non-Muslim submits.
• Slaves are a part of sacred war.
• Rape of captives is jihad.
• Assassination is a tactical strike of war.
• Killing of nonbelievers is to be done with a positive attitude.
• Theft is part of jihad.

Mohammed now attacked the last of the Jews in Medina. After a siege, the Jews surrendered. The women became slaves, the children were adopted as Muslims, and then 800 of the males were executed in the marketplace.

Assassins were sent to kill another Jew who had opposed Mohammed. The Koran condemned the Jews.

THE SOLUTION FOR THE JEWS

1684 That same day the angel Gabriel came to Mohammed at noon. He asked if Mohammed were through fighting. Gabriel and the angels were going to attack the last Jewish tribe in Medina. Gabriel said, "Allah commands you to go to the Jews. I am headed there now to shake their stronghold."

1684 So Mohammed called upon his troops and they headed to the forts of the Jews. Now the Jews of Medina lived in forts that were on the outskirts of Medina. Mohammed rode up to the forts and called out, "You brothers of apes, has Allah disgraced you and brought His vengeance upon you?"

1685-689 Mohammed put the Jews under siege for twenty-five days. Finally, the Jews offered to submit their fate to a Muslim, Abu, with whom they had had been an ally in the past. His judgment was simple. Kill all the men. Take their property and take the women and children as captives. Mohammed said, "You have given the judgment of Allah."

I690 The captives were taken into Medina. They dug trenches in the market place of Medina. It was a long day, but 800 Jews met their death that day. Mohammed and his twelve year old wife sat and watched the entire day and into the night. The Apostle of Allah had every male Jew killed.

I693 Mohammed took the property, wives and children of the Jews, and divided it up amongst the Muslims. Mohammed took his one fifth of the slaves and sent a Muslim with the female Jewish slaves to a nearby city where the women were sold for pleasure. Mohammed invested the money from the sale of the female slaves for horses and weapons.

I693 There was one last piece of spoils for Mohammed. The most beautiful Jewess was his slave for pleasure.

I696-7 In the battle of the Trench it was Allah who had won the day. Allah is what gives the Muslim his strength and will. No matter what the unbelievers do Allah will triumph. Allah totally approves of the killing of the Jews, enslaving the women and children. It was good to give the Jew's property to the Muslim warriors. After all, Allah wanted it done and helped to do it.

> 33:25 *And Allah drove back the unbelievers in their wrath, and they gained nothing by it. Allah aided the believers in the war, for Allah is strong and mighty. He brought down some of the People of the Book [the Jews] out of their fortresses to aid the confederates and to strike terror into their hearts. Some you killed, and others you took captive. He made you heirs of their land, their homes, and their possessions, and even gave you another land on which you had never before set foot. Allah has power over everything. [800 male Jews were executed, their property taken, and women and children enslaved.]*

THE KILLING OF THE JEW, SALLAM

I714-6 A Jew named Sallam helped to plan and organize the confederation of the tribes that attacked Mohammed in the Battle of the Trench. Mohammed sent five Muslim men to assassinate Sallam. When the men had done their work, they returned to Mohammed and fell to arguing as to who actually killed Sallam. Mohammed demanded to see their swords. He examined them one by one and then pointed to the sword that had been the killing weapon. It had food on it still from the thrust to the stomach.

The Koran's last words about the Jews:

> 5:13 *Because they [the Jews] broke their covenant, We have cursed them and have hardened their hearts. They changed the words of Scripture [Islam claims that the Jews removed the references to Mohammed's coming from their Scripture.] from their places and have forgotten part of what they were taught. You will always discover them in deceits, except for a few of them, but forgive them and overlook their misdeeds. Allah loves those who act generously.*
>
> 5:41 *Oh, Messenger, do not let those who hurry to disbelief grieve you. Whether it is those who say the words, "We believe," while their hearts do not believe, or, it is the Jews, who will listen to any lie but do not come to you. They change words from their contexts and say, "If you are given this, take it, if you are not given this, then beware of it." For whomever Allah would mislead, you will be no help for him against Allah. Those whose hearts Allah does not desire to cleanse will suffer disgrace in this world and a grievous punishment in the next.*
>
> 5:42 *They [the Jews] are fond of listening to lies or devouring anything forbidden. If they do come to you [Mohammed], judge between them, or refuse to interfere. If you withdraw from them, they cannot harm you in any way, but if you judge, then judge between them with equity. Allah loves those who deal equitably. Why would they make you their judge since they possess their own law, the Torah, which holds the commands of Allah, yet they have not obeyed it? These are not believers.*
>
> 5:44 *We have sent down the Torah, which was a guidance and light. The messengers who professed Islam used the Torah to judge the Jews, the rabbis, and the doctors because they were required to be the keepers and the witnesses of the Book. Therefore, Oh Jews, do not fear men but fear Me, and do not sell my signs for a miserable price. Whoever will not judge by what Allah revealed are the unbelievers.*
>
> 5:45 *We ordained in the Book, "Life for life, and eye for eye, and nose for nose, and ear for ear, and tooth for tooth, and for wounds retaliation." Whoever will give up retaliation, it is an act of atonement for his sins. Whoever does not use the laws of Allah to judge is unjust.*

The last sentence is a basis for the destruction of all non-Islamic political systems. Sharia law, the law of Allah, must replace all man-made laws, including the U.S. Constitution.

MOHAMMED'S FAMILY LIFE

CHAPTER 16

*48:13 We have prepared a blazing Fire for these unbelievers
who do not believe in Allah and His Messenger.*

• All Islamic family law is based upon Mohammed's family life.

When Mohammed went on his missions to attack those who resisted Islam, he took one of his wives with him. Which one got to go was determined by lots. Mohammed took Aisha with him on this trip to fight in Allah's cause in attacking the Mustaliq tribe.

I731 Now there was a problem in taking one of Mohammed's wives on an expedition and that was privacy. By now the veil had been prescribed for his wives. So the wife was not supposed to be seen or heard. To accomplish this a light cloth-covered howdah was used. Basically this was a box with a seat that could be mounted on a camel's saddle. On the way back on the expedition Aisha had gone out in the morning to relieve herself. When she got back she discovered that she had lost a necklace and went back to find it. The tent had been struck and the men in charge loaded the howdah on the camel and off they went without Aisha.

I732 When Aisha got back the entire group had moved on. She returned on a camel lead by a young Muslim who had lagged behind the main body and brought her back to Medina.

I732 Tongues began to wag, imaginations worked overtime and gossip spread. Aisha fell ill and was bedridden for three weeks.

I734-5 Tempers flared and men offered to kill the gossips. Something had to be done. In the end the innocence or guilt of Aisha was determined by revelation in the Koran which to this day is the sharia (Islamic law) about adultery.

> 24:11 *Truly there is a group among you who spread that lie [During an armed raid, Aisha—Mohammed's favorite wife since their marriage when she was age six—accidentally spent a day alone with a young jihadist. Gossip about what might have happened consumed the Muslims], but do not think of it as a bad thing for you [Aisha was cleared of doubt of sexual infidelity by a revelation in the Koran] for it has*

proved to be advantageous for you. Every one of them will receive the punishment they have earned. Those who spread the gossip will receive a torturous punishment.

24:12 *Why did the believing men and women, when they heard this, not think better of their own people and say, "This is an obvious lie"? Why did they not bring four witnesses? And because they could not find any witnesses, they are surely liars in Allah's sight.*

Since there were not four witnesses, then there was no adultery and the gossips got eighty lashes.

1736 But the scandal did not end here. One of those who got flogged for gossip was a poet and propagandist for the Muslim cause. The young warrior who led Aisha's camel was in a poem written by the poet and was offended. So he took his sword and cut the poet badly. The poet and his friends managed to bind the young warrior and take him to Mohammed. Mohammed wanted this to all go away. He gave the wounded poet a nice home and a Christian slave girl of pleasure as compensation for the sword blow.

Islam was no longer poor, indeed, the money from jihad poured in. But Mohammed was a simple man and had no attraction to money. Hence, his household was poor and the wives complained.

33:28 *Messenger! Say to your wives, "If you desire a life of this world and all its glittering adornment, then come. [All of the money from the spoils of war was spent on support of the Muslims and jihad. Mohammed's wives complained about the lack of household money.] I will provide for you and release you with honor. If, however, you seek Allah and His Messenger and the world to come, then know that Allah has prepared a great reward for those of you who do good works.*

33:50 *Messenger! We allow you your wives whose dowries you have paid, and the slave-girls Allah has granted you as spoils of war, and the daughters of your paternal and maternal uncles and aunts who fled with you to Medina, and any believing woman who gives herself to the Messenger, if the Messenger wishes to marry her. This is a privilege for you only, not for any other believer. We know what We have commanded the believers concerning wives and slave-girls. We give you this privilege so you will be free from blame. Allah is forgiving and merciful!*

MARY, THE COPTIC SLAVE OF PLEASURE

M425 Mohammed was given two Coptic (Egyptian Christian) slaves. One he gave to another Muslim but he kept Mary, fair of skin with curly hair. He did not move her into the harem, but set up an apartment in another part of Medina. Mary gave something in sex that none of his wives could—a child and it was a male child, Ibrahim. Mohammed doted on him.

M426 The harem was jealous. This non-Arab slave had given Mohammed his best gift. One of his wives, Hafsa, was away and Mohammed took Mary to Hafsa's apartment in the harem. Hafsa returned and there was a scene. The harem was incensed. A slave in one of their beds was an outrage and a scandal. The wives banded together and it was a house of anger and coldness.

M427 Mohammed withdrew and swore he would not see his wives for a month and lived with Mary. Omar and Abu Bakr were appalled as Mohammed, their son-in-law had abandoned their daughters for a slave. But at last Mohammed relented and said that Gabriel had spoken well of Hafsa and he wanted the whole affair to be over.

> 66:1 *Why, Oh, Messenger, do you forbid yourself that which Allah has made lawful to you? Do you seek to please your wives? [Mohammed was fond of a Coptic (Egyptian Christian) slave named Mary. Hafsa found Mohammed in her room with Mary, a violation of Hafsa's domain. He told a jealous Hafsa that he would stop relations with Mary and then did not. But Hafsa was supposed to be quiet about this matter.] Allah is lenient and merciful. Allah has allowed you release from your oaths, and Allah is your master. He is knowing and wise.*
>
> 66:3 *When the Messenger confided a fact to one of his wives, and when she divulged it, [Hafsa had told Aisha (Mohammed's favorite wife) about Mary and the harem became embroiled in jealousy.] Allah informed Mohammed of this, and he told her [Hafsa] part of it and withheld part. When Mohammed told her of it, she said, "Who told you this?" He said, "He who is knowing and wise told me."*
>
> 66:4 *"If you both [Hafsa and Aisha] turn in repentance to Allah, your hearts are already inclined to this, but if you conspire against the Messenger, then know that Allah is his protector, and Gabriel, and every just man among the faithful, and the angels are his helpers besides. Perhaps, if he [Mohammed] divorced you all, Allah would give him better wives than you—Muslims, believers, submissive, devout, penitent, obedient, observant of fasting, widows, and virgins."*

M429 Ibrahim became a favorite of Mohammed. But when the child was fifteen months old, he fell sick. Mary and her slave sister attended the child during his illness. Mohammed was there at his death and wept mightily. Mohammed was to suffer the Arabic shame of having no living male children to succeed him.

MARRIAGE TO HIS DAUGHTER-IN-LAW

M290 Mohammed had an adopted son, Zeid, and went by his house. Zeid was not there and Mohammed went on in the house. He wound up seeing his daughter-in-law, Zeinab, in a thin dress, and her charms were evident. Mohammed was smitten and said, "Gracious Lord! Good Heavens! How thou dost turn the hearts of men!"

M290 Well, Zeinab, had turned the head of the future king of Arabia and she told her husband what Mohammed said. The step-son went to Mohammed and said that he would divorce Zeinab so he could have her. Mohammed said no. But Zeid went ahead and divorced her anyway. In Arabia a union between a man and his daughter-in-law was incest and forbidden. But while Mohammed was with Aisha, he had a revelation and said, "Who will go and congratulate Zeinab and tell her that Allah has blessed our marriage?" The maid went right off to tell her of the good news. So Mohammed added another wife.

> 33:4 *Allah has not given any man two hearts for one body, nor has He made your wives whom you divorce to be like your mothers, nor has He made your adopted sons like your real sons. [Previous to this verse, an Arab's adopted children were treated as blood children. This verse relates to verse 37 of this sura.] These are only words you speak with your mouths, but Allah speaks the truth and guides to the right path. Name your adopted sons after their real fathers; this is more just in Allah's sight. But if you do not know their fathers' names, call them your brothers in the faith and your friends. There will be no blame on you if you sin unintentionally, but that which you intend in your heart will be held against you. Allah is forgiving and merciful.*
>
> 33:36 *And it is not the place of a believer, either man or woman, to have a choice in his or her affairs when Allah and His Messenger have decided on a matter. Those who disobey Allah and His Messenger are clearly on the wrong path. And remember when you said to your adopted son [Zayd], the one who had received Allah's favor [converted to Islam], "Keep your wife to yourself and fear Allah," and you hid in your heart what Allah was to reveal, and you feared men [what people would say if he married his daughter-in-law], when it would have been right that you should fear Allah. And when Zayd divorced his wife, We gave her to you as your wife, so it would not be a sin for believers to marry the wives of their adopted sons, after they have divorced them. And Allah's will must be carried out.*

Since Zeid was adopted, he was not really a son, so there was no incest.

JIHAD, THE FIRST DHIMMIS

CHAPTER 17

4:80 Those who obey the Messenger, obey Allah. As for those who turn away from you, We have not sent you to watch over them.

- Torture is part of jihad.
- Non-Muslims can be used as semi-slaves for Islam.
- Non-Muslims have few rights under Islamic law.
- Non-Muslims can be taxed at a higher rate than Muslims.
- Terror is part of jihad.
- Non-Muslims submit to Islam to avoid violence.
- Violence advances Islam.

Mohammed now had a treaty with the Meccans and he turned his attention the Jews who lived in Khaybar, a town two days from Medina.

Mohammed captured the Jewish forts and signed a treaty with the Jews so that they became semi-slaves called *dhimmis.* The Jews would work the land and give half of the profits to Mohammed.

He took their wealth and took the most beautiful Jewess as his wife.

The Jews of Fadak panicked and surrendered to become dhimmis and gave Mohammed their wealth.

THE TREATY OF AL HUDAYBIYA

1740 Mohammed decided to make a pilgrimage to Mecca. A difficult problem was how to do this peacefully. The state of affairs between Mohammed and the Meccans had always condemnation and violence.

1741 As they approached Mecca, he found out that the Quraysh had come out prepared for war and were blocking the way. So Mohammed took an alternate and difficult route to Mecca and try to avoid the armed Meccans.

1743 The Meccans were not going to let him enter, war or no war. They would not submit to Mohammed's wishes. They would not lose face with the other Arabs.

1747 The Meccans set a man out to parlay and make a treaty with Mohammed. Umar was furious that Mohammed would even make a treaty with non-Muslims. To make a treaty with non-Muslims was demeaning to Islam. But Mohammed told him that Allah would not make them the loser. They would win over the Quraysh. Be patient.

1747 So they drew up a treaty to the effect that there would be no war for ten years, there would be no hostilities, no one could convert to Islam without their guardians' permission. In turn the Muslims could come next year and stay for three days in Mecca, but they could not enter this year.

1748 Many of the Muslims were depressed. Mohammed had promised that they could enter Mecca. Now they could not. Before they left they sacrificed the camels and shaved their heads doing as much of the rituals they could without getting into Mecca.

1750 This was a victory for Islam. The government of Mecca dealt with Mohammed as an independent political power. Many more Arabs were attracted to Islam with its new power.

1754 The treaty greatly enhanced the Islam's political power.

KHAYBAR

1756 After the treaty of Al Hudaybiya, Mohammed stayed in Medina for about two months before he collected his army and marched to the forts of Khaybar, a community of wealthy Jewish farmers who lived in a village of separate forts about 100 miles from Medina.

1758 Mohammed seized the forts one at a time. Among the captives was a beautiful Jewess named Safiya. Mohammed took her for his sexual pleasure. One of his men had first chosen her for his own slave of pleasure, but Mohammed traded him two of her cousins for Safiya. Mohammed always got first choice of the spoils of war and the women.

1759 On the occasion of Khaybar, Mohammed put forth new orders about the sex with captive women. If the woman was pregnant, she was not to be used for sex until after the birth of the child. Nor were any women to be used for sex who were unclean with regards to the Muslim laws about menstruation.

1764 Mohammed knew that there was a large treasure hidden somewhere in Khaybar, so he brought forth the Jew who he thought knew the most about it and questioned him. The Jew denied any knowledge. Mohammed told one of his men, "Torture the Jew until you extract what he has." So the Jew was staked on the ground, and a small fire built on his chest to get him to talk. When the man was nearly dead and still would not talk, Mohammed had him released and taken to one of his men who had had a brother killed in the fight. This Muslim got the pleasure of cutting off the tortured Jew's head.

1764 At Khaybar Mohammed instituted the first dhimmis. After the best of the goods were taken from the Jews Mohammed left them to work the land. Since his men knew nothing about farming, and the Jews were skilled at it, they worked the land and gave Mohammed half of their profits.

1774 There were a total of 1,800 people who divided up the wealth taken from the beaten Jews of Khaybar. A cavalry man got three shares, a foot soldier got one share. Mohammed appointed eighteen chiefs to divide the loot. Mohammed received his one-fifth before it was distributed.

FADAK

1777 The Jews of Fadak panicked when they saw what Mohammed did at Khaybar. They would be next, so they surrendered to Mohammed without a fight. Since there was no battle Mohammed got 100% of their goods and they worked the land and gave half to Mohammed each year. They became dhimmis like those of Khaybar.

MOHAMMED'S FINAL JIHAD

CHAPTER 18

*3:53 "Our Lord! We believe in what Thou hast
revealed, and we follow the Apostle; then write
us down among those who bear witness."*

- Jihad is an ongoing, constant process.
- Non-Muslims will submit to Islam when enough violence is used.
- Art of non-Muslims can be destroyed.
- The principles of Islam are the basis of law. Nonbelievers must submit to Islamic law.
- The law of non-Muslims must be replaced with Islamic law.
- Ancient religious sites are to be destroyed.
- Non-Muslims may buy the protection of Islam (the *jizya*).
- A jihadist kills with enthusiasm.
- Islam must dominate all public space.
- Jihad is demanded of all Muslims, except the old and sick.
- All Muslims should donate money for jihad.
- Islam sets the standards and rules for all other religions in Islamic lands.

Mohammed continued his jihad against all non-Muslim economic targets. A year after his treaty with the Meccans, the Muslims went on their pilgrimage to Mecca.

The Muslims lost the battle at Muta against a Byzantine army.

Trouble flared up with an ally of the Meccans, and Mohammed used this as a reason to send an army to Mecca. This time the Meccans surrendered to an Islam strengthened since the treaty.

Mohammed entered Mecca, took political control, destroyed all art and issued death warrants against every artist and opponent.

Mohammed continued his war against the non-Muslims. His last jihad to Tabuk did not go well as many Muslims did not want to go on the difficult campaign.

The Koran spoke at length against Muslims who do not follow the command for jihad. Jihad is eternal and for all Muslims.

Abu Bakr lead the pilgrimage to Mecca. Mecca was now only for Muslims. Many tribes now submitted to Islam as they saw where the new political power lay.

THE PILGRIMAGE

1789 After returning from Khaybar, Mohammed sent out many raiding parties and expeditions. Seven years after Mohammed moved to Medina and one year after the treaty of Hudaybiya, Mohammed led the Muslims to the Kabah in Mecca. While there he kissed one of the stones of the Kabah and trotted around the Kabah. When he got to the corner with the Black Stone, he walked up and kissed it. He did this for three circuits of the Kabah.

1789 As Mohammed entered Mecca, the man leading his camel said this poetry:

> Get out of his way, unbelievers, make way
> I know Allah's truth in accepting it
> We will fight you about its interpretation
> As we have fought you about its revelation
> We will cut off your head and remove friend from friend.

1790 After his three day stay in Mecca, the Quraysh asked him to leave as per the treaty. Mohammed asked to stay and have a wedding feast and he would invite the Quraysh. The Quraysh said no, please leave. He left.

THE RAID ON MUTA

1791-3 Mohammed sent an army of 3000 to Muta soon after his return from Mecca. Now Muta was north of Medina, near Syria. When they arrived the Muslims found a large army of the Byzantines. They argued about what to do. One of them said, "Men, you are complaining of what you came here to do. Die as martyrs. Islam does not fight with numbers or strength but with Islam. Come! We have only two prospects. Victory or martyrdom, both are fine. Let us go forward!"

1796 The Muslims were cut to ribbons. The Byzantines were professionals and superior in numbers.

1798 The Muslims who remained behind in Medina scorned the returning fighters. They threw dirt at them and said, "You are runaways. You fled from the way of Allah. You fled from jihad." Poetry was written to the effect that the men kept their distance from the Byzantine army and were afraid of death. They loved life too much and feared death.

MECCA CONQUERED

1803 At the treaty of Hudaybiya, it was agreed that the Meccans and Mohammed could make alliances between themselves and other tribes. There were two different Arab tribes, one allied with the Meccans and the other allied with Mohammed. As tribes are prone to do, there was a murder and subsequently retaliation by the other tribe. Then it was escalated by the Quraysh of Mecca when they helped out their ally. A chief came to Mohammed to tell of his losses and how it was time for Mohammed to take the cause of his ally and punish the Quraysh of Mecca.

1811 As a result of the fighting between a tribe allied with the Meccans and a tribe allied with Mohammed, he marched on Mecca with 10,000 men to punish them.

1813 The Muslims camped at a small town near Mecca. The Meccans needed to know whether Mohammed was going to enter Mecca. Many lives would be saved if the people would come out and seek protection, so they would not be killed.

1813-4 The chief of the Muslims, Abu Sufyan, came to the Muslim camp to negotiate. Abu Sufyan, the chief Meccan, spent the night in the Muslim army camp and went to Mohammed the next morning. Mohammed spoke, "Isn't it time for you to recognize that there is no god but Allah?" Abu answered, "I thought that there had been another god with Allah, he would have helped me." Mohammed replied, "Woe to you, Abu Sufyan, is it not time to recognize that I am Allah's apostle?" Abu Sufyan said, "As to that I have some doubt." He was told, "Submit and testify that there is no god but Allah and that Mohammed is his apostle before you lose your head!" So he submitted.

Abu Sufyan went ahead and announced to Mecca that Mohammed's army was coming. They were not to resist but to go into their houses, his house or the Kabah and that they would be safe.

1819 Mohammed had told his commanders only to kill those who resisted. Otherwise they were to bother no one except for those who had spoken against Mohammed. The list of those to be killed:

- One of Mohammed's secretaries, who had said that when he was recording Mohammed's Koranic revelations sometimes Mohammed let the secretary insert better speech. This caused him to lose faith and he became an apostate.

- Two singing girls who had sung satires against Mohammed.
- A Muslim tax collector who had become an apostate (left Islam).
- A man who had insulted Mohammed.

I821 Mohammed went to the Kabah and rode around it seven times. Each time he went past the Black Stone, he touched it with his stick. Then he called for the key to the Kabah and entered. There was a wooden dove carved that he picked up and broke and threw out the door. There were 360 ritual objects representing the gods of the various Arab faiths. Mohammed had them all destroyed by burning.

Mohammed announced the end of all feuds, all revenge killings, payment of blood money. Veneration of the ancestors was over.

KHALID'S DESTRUCTION OF THE NATIVE SHRINE

I840 Mohammed sent Khalid to an ancient temple near Mecca that was used by several tribes for worship. When Khalid got there, he destroyed it completely.

THE BATTLE OF HUNAIN

I840 When Mohammed took Mecca, the surrounding Arab tribes saw that if he was not opposed he would be King of Arabia. The Hawazin Arabs decided to oppose him under the leadership of Malik.

I842 Mohammed sent a spy to gather intelligence about the Arabs. When he received the information, he set about for jihad. He first borrowed armor and lances from a wealthy Meccan and then marched out with 12,000 men.

I845 When the army descended into the broad area, they found the enemy prepared and hiding, waiting to attack. The Muslim troops broke and ran. Mohammed stood in his stirrups and called out, "Where are you going? Come to me, the Apostle of Allah." Most of the men continued to retreat except his battle hardened core troops who regrouped around him. About a core of 100 lead the charge to turn the tide. They were steadfast. Mohammed looked at the carnage and said, "Now the oven is hot!"

I847 One of the Muslim women was near Mohammed and said about those who were retreating, "Kill those who flee just as you kill those who are attacking us."

9:25 *Allah has helped you in many battlefields, and on the day of Hunain, when your great numbers elated you [there were 12,000 Muslims and 4000 unbelievers], but availed you nothing [the Muslims panicked and fled], and the earth, for all its breadth, constrained you, you turned your backs in flight.*

THE RAID ON TABUK

1894 Mohammed decided to raid the Byzantines. Normally he never let his men actually know where he was headed. He would announce a destination, but after they were on the way, he would announce the actual place. But this raid was far away in very hot weather, so greater preparations would need to be made. The men began to prepare, but with no enthusiasm due to the heat, it was time for harvest to begin and they remembered the last combat with the Byzantines—they lost badly.

1894 When Mohammed asked one of his best men if he wanted to go, the man replied, "Would you allow me to stay? You know how much I love women and when I see the Byzantine women, I don't know if I will be able to control myself." So Mohammed told him to stay. But the Koran had a comment:

> 9:45 *The only ones who will ask leave of you are those who do not believe in Allah and the Last Day, whose hearts are full of doubts, and who waver in their doubts. If they had intended to go to war, they would have prepared for war. But Allah was opposed to their marching forth and held them back. It was said, "Sit at home with those who sit." If they had taken the field with you, they would not have added to your strength but would have hurried about among you, stirring up dissension. Some of you would have listened to them. Allah knows the evildoers. They had plotted dissension before and made plots against you again until the truth arrived. Then the decree of Allah prevailed, much to their disgust.*
> 9:49 *Some of them say to you, "Allow me to remain at home, and do not expose me to temptation." Have they not already fallen into temptation? Hell will surround the unbelievers. If a success befalls you [Mohammed], it annoys them. If a misfortune befalls you, they say, "We took our precautions," and they turn their backs and are glad.*

1895 There was much grumbling about the heat.

> 9:81 *Those who were left behind were delighted at sitting behind Allah's Messenger. They hated to strive and fight with their riches and their lives for Allah's cause [jihad] and said, "Do not go out in the heat." Say: The Fire of Hell is a fiercer heat." If they would only understand. Let them laugh a little for they will weep much in payment for their deeds.*
> 9:83 *If Allah brings you back from the fight and they ask your permission to march out with you the next time, say, "You will never come out with*

me or fight an enemy with me. You were well pleased to sit at home at the first crisis, so sit at home with those who lag behind."

1896 So Mohammed set off, but there were many Muslims who were slow to leave or they came with misgivings. After the first camp some of the Muslims left and returned to Medina. These were called hypocrites.

1902 When they got to Tabuk, the people there paid the poll tax, *jizya*. By paying the poll tax, a per person tax, they would not be attacked, killed or robbed by the Muslims. Those who paid the jizya were under the protection of Islam

1903 Mohammed sent Khalid to the fort of a Christian chief. When the chief and his brother rode out of their fort to inspect the cattle, Khalid killed the chief's brother and captured the ruler. The chief agreed to pay the poll tax to Islam. Mohammed returned to Medina.

The Battle of Tabuk was hard for Mohammed. The Muslims did not come out to be jihadists as they had before. But the Koran makes clear that jihad is an obligation.

> 9:85 *Do not let their riches or their children astonish you. Through these Allah is inclined to punish them in this world and to let their souls depart while they are still unbelievers. When a sura [chapter] was sent down saying, "Believe in Allah and strive and go to war with His Messenger," those of them who are possessed of riches demanded exemption saying, "Leave us behind that we may be with those who sit at home." They are well contented to be with those who stay behind for their hearts are sealed. They do not understand.*

> 9:93 *The cause for blame is only against those who ask for exemption though they are rich. They are pleased to be with those who stay behind, and Allah has set a seal upon their hearts so they do not know. They will present their excuses to you when you return to them. Say: Do not present excuses. We cannot believe you. Allah has informed us about you. Allah and His Messenger will behold your doings. You will return to the knower of the seen and the unseen. He will tell you the truth of what you have done.*

ETERNAL JIHAD

M448 After all the victories, some Muslims said that the days of fighting were over and even began to sell their arms. But Mohammed forbid this, saying, "There shall not cease from the midst of my people a party engaged in fighting for the truth, until the Antichrist appears." Jihad was recognized as the normal state of affairs. Indeed, the Koran prepares the way for this:

9:122 *The faithful should not all go out together to fight. If a part of every troop remained behind, they could instruct themselves in their religion and warn their people when they return to them that they should guard against evil.*

9:123 *Believers, fight the unbelievers who are near you, and let them find you to be tough and hard. Know that Allah is with those who guard against evil.*

ABU BAKR LEADS THE PILGRIMAGE

1919-20 Abu Bakr led the pilgrimage from Medina to Mecca. While they were in Mecca major changes were made to the treaty of Hudaybiya, which are recorded in the Koran. The treaty is only good for four more months, then jihad will be declared if the non-Muslims don't submit to Islam.

1922 After this time, those who practice the old native religions of Arabia will no longer be able to come to Mecca for pilgrimage.

1924 The non-Muslims are unclean and must not approach the Kabah. The money that will be lost from their pilgrimages will be taken care of by Allah. Jihad will bring in the lost money.

9:28 *Oh, believers, only the unbelievers are unclean. Do not let them come near the Sacred Temple after this year of theirs. If you fear poverty from the loss of their business [breaking commercial ties with the Meccans], Allah will enrich you from His abundance if He pleases. Allah is knowing and wise.*

1924 The Koran then turns to the issue of the raid on the Byzantines at Tabuk. Muslims must answer the call to jihad. It is an obligation. If the Byzantine raid had been short and had made for easy war spoils, the Muslims would have joined readily. But instead they made excuses. A Muslim's duty is not to avoid fighting with their person and money.

9:38 *Oh, believers, what possessed you that when it was said, "March forth in Allah's cause [jihad]," you cling heavily to the earth? Do you prefer the life of this world to the next? Little is the comfort of this life compared to the one that is to come. Unless you march forth, He will punish you with a grievous penalty, and He will put another in your place. You will not harm Him at all, for Allah has power over everything.*

9:40 *If you do not assist your Messenger, it is no matter for Allah assisted him when the unbelievers drove him out, he [Mohammed] being only one of two men. When the two [Mohammed and Abu Bakr] were in the cave, the Messenger said to his companion, "Do not be distressed, for Allah is with us." Allah sent His tranquility upon him, and strengthened him with hosts you did not see. He humbled the word of those who disbelieved and exalted the word of Allah, for Allah is mighty and wise. March forth both the lightly and heavily armed, and strive hard in Allah's cause [jihad] with your substance and your persons. This is better for you if you know it.*

9:42 *Had there been a near advantage and a short journey [Mohammed marched to Tabuk against the Greeks. It was a long, hot campaign], they would certainly have followed you, but the journey was too long for them. Yet they will swear by Allah saying, "If we only could have, we would surely have gone forth with you." They would destroy their own souls. Allah knows that they are surely lying.*

9:43 *Allah forgive you, Mohammed. Why did you give them permission to stay behind before you knew those who told the truth from those who lied? Those who believe in Allah and in the Last Day do not ask for exemption from fighting with their wealth and their lives. Allah knows those who fear Him.*

1926 Those who try to avoid jihad are hypocrites. The Prophet should struggle against them. They are bound for Hell.

9:73 *Oh, Prophet, strive hard against the unbelievers and the hypocrites, and be firm with them. Hell will be their dwelling place: A wretched journey.*

Those who believe in Allah and the Apostle and enter jihad with their wealth and selves will prosper and enter Paradise. This is a promise from Allah.

1933 When Mohammed had taken Mecca and Tabuk, deputations began to come from the Arabs. The Arabs were waiting to see what would happen between the Quraysh and Mohammed. When Mohammed was victorious, the Arabs came in groups and joined with him.

1956 The kings of Himyar wrote to Mohammed that they had submitted to Islam. Mohammed wrote them back, "... I received your message and am informed of your Islam and your killing non-Muslims. Allah has guided you. ... send the one fifth of the spoils of war and tax the believers... Christians and Jews who do not convert must pay the poll tax..."

1965 Mohammed sent out tax collectors to every part of Islam to collect the tax.

MOHAMMED'S LAST YEAR

CHAPTER 19

24:51 But when Allah and His Messenger call
the true believers to judge between them, their
response is, "We have heard, and we obey."

- All religions must submit to Islam.
- Islam determines the doctrine of all religions.
- Mohammed was the perfect jihadist.
- Mohammed was involved in all aspects of slavery.
- Islam succeeds through violence.

Mohammed took his last pilgrimage to Mecca and gave his last sermon.

The final state of Christians and Jews is subservience to Islam. Islam defines both Christianity and Judaism. Both religions have corrupt sacred texts.

After averaging a violent event every six weeks for nine years, Mohammed died.

THE FAREWELL PILGRIMAGE

1968 Ten years after entering Medina Mohammed made what was to be his last pilgrimage to Mecca. There he made his farewell address. He told the Muslims that usury was abolished, Allah would judge them and their works. All of the blood shed before Islam was to be left unavenged. The lunar calendar was the sacred calendar and it was not to be adjusted with respect to the solar calendar.

1969 The men have rights over their wives and the wives have rights over the men. The wives must never commit adultery nor act in a sexual manner towards others. If they do, put them in separate rooms and beat them lightly. If they refrain from these things, they have the right to food and clothing. Lay injunctions on women lightly for they are prisoners of the men and have no control over their persons.

M473 Feed and clothe your slaves well.

1969 Every Muslim is a Muslim's brother. Only take from a brother what he gives you.

1970 Mohammed led the Muslims through the rituals of the pilgrimage.

THE FINAL STATE OF CHRISTIANS AND JEWS

M453 When Mohammed first started preaching in Mecca, his religion was Arabian. Then Allah became identified with Jehovah and Jewish elements were introduced. When Mohammed moved to Medina, he argued with the Jews when they denied his status as a prophet in the Judaic line. He then annihilated the Jews and makes no more connections between Islam and the Jews. In his last statement, Jews and Christians became perpetual second class political citizens, dhimmis (pay the dhimmi tribute, jizya, and are subdued). Only those Christians and Jews who submit to Islam are protected. Islam defines Judaism and Christianity. The real Christians are those who deny the Trinity and accept Mohammed as the final prophet. The real Jews are those who accept Mohammed as the final prophet of their god, Jehovah. Both Christians and Jews must accept that the Koran is the true Scripture and that the Old Testament and New Testament are corrupt and in error. The contradictions between the Koran and the New and Old Testament are proof of the corruption of the nonbelievers.

All other Jews and Christians are false and unbelievers.

> 9:29 *Make war on those who have received the Scriptures [Jews and Christians] but do not believe in Allah or in the Last Day. They do not forbid what Allah and His Messenger have forbidden. The Christians and Jews do not follow the religion of truth until they submit and pay the poll tax [jizya], and they are humiliated.*

The Christians have hidden their prophesies that Mohammed would come to fulfill the work of Christ. To believe in the divinity of Christ is to refuse to submit to Islam. Those Christians are unbelievers and infidels. Like the Jews, only those Christians who submit to Islam and become dhimmis and are ruled by the sharia (Islamic law) are actual Christians. Islam defines all religions. No religion defines itself, except Islam.

> 5:14 *We made a covenant with those who say, "We are Christians," but they, too, have forgotten a part of what they were taught [Islam claims that the Christians suppressed the prophecies of Jesus that Mohammed would be the final prophet] so We have stirred up animosity and hatred among them that will last until Resurrection Day. In the end, Allah will tell them what they have done.*

5:15 *Oh, people of the Scriptures, Our Messenger has come to you to clear up what you have hidden of those Scriptures and to pass over many things that are now unnecessary. Now you have a new light and a clear Book from Allah. He will use it to guide whoever seeks to follow His good pleasure to paths of peace. He will bring them out of the darkness to the light, and, by his decree, will guide them to the straight path.*
5:17 *Surely they are unbelievers who say, "Allah is the Messiah, son of Mary." Say: Who has any power against Allah if He chose to destroy the Messiah, son of Mary, his mother, and all who are on the earth together? Allah's is the sovereignty of the heavens and of the earth and of all that is between them. He creates what He will, and Allah has power over all things.*

A SUMMARY OF MOHAMMED'S ARMED EVENTS

1973 In a nine year period Mohammed personally attended twenty-seven raids. There were thirty-eight other battles and expeditions. This is a total of sixty-five armed events, not including assassinations and executions, for an average of one armed event every seven weeks.

MOHAMMED'S DEATH

I1000 When Mohammed spoke to Aisha, his favorite wife, she complained of a headache. Mohammed said, "No, Aisha, Oh my head. Would it distress you if you were to die before me so that I might wrap you in your shroud and pray over you?" Aisha said, "I think that if you did that, that after you returned to the house you would simply spend the night with one of your other wives." But the pain became worse and he took his final illness in the house of Aisha.

I1006 Mohammed weakened and was in a great deal of pain. Later he died with his head in Aisha's lap. His final words were the perfect summation of Islam, political action based upon religion.

> B4,52,288 *Mohammed said, "There should not be two religions no other religions besides Islam in Arabia" and that the money should be continued to be paid to influence the foreign, unbeliever ambassadors.*

T1831 Mohammed was buried beneath his bed. The bed was removed and a grave was dug where the bed had stood.

JIHAD, CONQUEST

CHAPTER 20

*8:13 This was because they opposed Allah and
His messenger. Ones who oppose Allah and His
messenger will be severely punished by Allah.*

After Mohammed's death, Abu Bakr was elected caliph (political and
religious leader) to rule over Islam. He went to war against the many Muslims who wished to leave Islam after Mohammed's death. Thousands of
these apostates were killed in the Riddah wars, the war against apostasy.
The rule of political Islam in Arabia was now permanent.

Umar became the next caliph and put Mohammed's final command
into effect by expelling every Christian and Jew in Arabia. To this day there
is no temple, church, synagogue, shrine or any house of worship except
that of Islam in Arabia. Umar then launched the jihad and conquest of every neighbor of Arabia. The Islamic Empire was born and political Islam
became a permanent part of world politics.

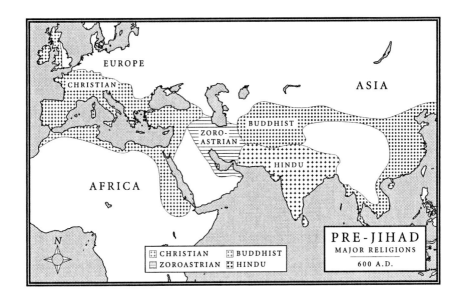

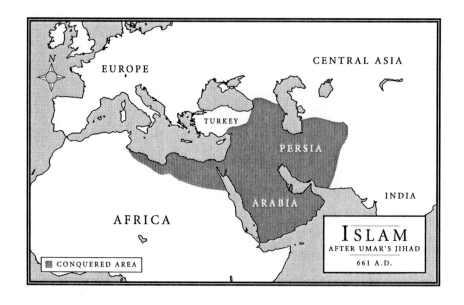

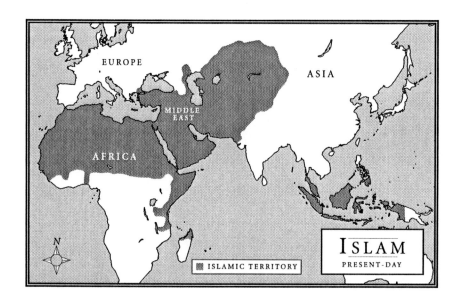

ETHICS

CHAPTER 21

*9:63 Do they not know that whoever opposes Allah
and His Messenger will abide in the fire of Hell, where
they will remain forever? This is the great shame.*

Outsiders judge a religion by its ethics. They are not concerned with
what it teaches about salvation or life after death, but they care greatly
what the religion tells members about outsiders. The foundation of this
interaction between adherents and non-members is ethics.

The Hadith is filled with details of the ethics of Islam.

BROTHERHOOD

The brother of a Muslim is another Muslim.

B1,2,12 Mohammed: "True faith comes when a man's personal desires
mirror his wishes for other Muslims."

B8,73,99 Mohammed: "Worshipers of Allah, do not allow hatred or jeal-
ousy to divide you. Live as brothers. It is sacrilege for one Muslim to desert
his brother or to refuse to speak with him for three successive nights."

B9,85,83 Mohammed: "A Muslim is a brother to other Muslims. He should
never oppress them nor should he facilitate their oppression. Allah will
satisfy the needs of those who satisfy the needs of their brothers."

HONESTY

A Muslim should always be honest in dealing with other Muslims.

B3,34,301 A man selling wares in the market place swore by Allah that he
had been offered a certain price for his goods when, in fact, no such offer
existed. He lied about the offer to drive up the price for his goods and thus
cheat a fellow Muslim. Consequently, this verse in the Koran was revealed
to Mohammed:

> 3:77 *Those who sell their covenant with Allah and their oaths for a
> meager price will have no part in the world to come. Allah will not
> find them worthy to speak to or even glance in their direction on*

the Day of Resurrection, nor will He forgive them. They will have
a painful end.

B1,2,54 Jirir promised Mohammed that he would strictly follow prayer ritual, pay his taxes to help the needy, and be faithful and truthful to all Muslims.

TRUTH

In Islam something that is not true is not always a lie.

B3,49,857 Mohammed: "A man who brings peace to the people by making up good words or by saying nice things, though untrue, does not lie."

An oath by a Muslim is flexible.

B8,78,618 Abu Bakr faithfully kept his oaths until Allah revealed to Mohammed the atonement for breaking them. Afterwards he said, "If I make a pledge and later discover a more worthy pledge, then I will take the better action and make amends for my earlier promise."

When deception advances Islam, the deception is not a sin.

B5,59,369 Mohammed asked, "Who will kill Ka'b, the enemy of Allah and Mohammed?"

Bin Maslama rose and responded, "O Mohammed! Would it please you if I killed him?"

Mohammed answered, "Yes."

Bin Maslama then said, "Give me permission to deceive him with lies so that my plot will succeed."

Mohammed replied, "You may speak falsely to him."

Ali was raised by Mohammed from the age of ten and became the fourth caliph. Ali pronounced the following on lies and deception.

B9,84,64 When I relate to you the words of Mohammed, by Allah, I would rather die than bear false witness to his teachings. However, if I should say something unrelated to the prophet, then it might very well be a lie so that I might deceive my enemy. Without question, I heard Mohammed say, "In the final days before Redemption there will emerge groups of foolish youths who will say all the right things but their faith will go no further than their mouths and will flee from their religion like an arrow. So, kill the apostates wherever you find them, because whoever does so will be rewarded on Judgment Day."

Deceit is part of Islamic war against the nonbelievers.

B4,52,267 Mohammed: "The king of Persia will be destroyed, and no one shall assume his throne. Caesar will certainly be destroyed and no Caesar will follow him; his coffers will be spent in Allah's cause." Mohammed cried out, "Jihad is deceit."

Deceit in war:

M032,6303 According to Mohammed, someone who strives to promote harmony amongst the faithful and says or conveys good things is not a liar. Ibn Shihab said that he had heard only three exceptions to the rules governing false statements: lies are permissible in war, to reconcile differences between the faithful, and to reconcile a husband and wife through the manipulation or twisting of words.

The name for deception that advances Islam is taqiyya *(safeguard, concealment, piety). But a Muslim must never lie to another Muslim. A lie should never be told unless there is no other way to accomplish the task Al Tabarani, in* Al Awsat, *said, "Lies are sins except when they are told for the welfare of a Muslim or for saving him from a disaster."* [1]

LAW

The hadiths are the basis of the Sharia, Islamic law. Here is a hadith about capital crimes. Killing a non-Muslim is not a capital crime.

B1,3,111 I [Abu] asked Ali, "Do you know of any sources of law that were revealed to Mohammed other than the Koran?" Ali responded, "None except for Allah's law, or the ability of reason given by Allah to a Muslim, or these written precepts I possess." I said, "What are these written rules?" Ali answered, "They concern the blood money paid by a killer to a victim's relatives, the method of ransoming a captive's release from the enemy, and the law that a Muslim must never be killed as punishment for killing a non-Muslim."

---

1. Bat Ye'or, *The Dhimmi* (Cranbury, N.J.: Associated University Presses, 2003), 392.

TREATMENT OF FELLOW MUSLIMS

Do not harm another Muslim.

B1,2,9 Mohammed: "The difference between a Muslim and an Immigrant[1] is that a Muslim avoids harming other Muslims with words or deeds, while an Immigrant merely abandons everything that Allah forbids."

Weapons in the mosque are acceptable. The mosque is a political center as well as a community center and a place of worship.

B1,8,443 Mohammed: "Arrows should be held by their heads when carried through mosques or markets so that they do not harm a Muslim."

In business, a Muslim should never cheat a Muslim.

B9,86,109 Mohammed said, "A neighbor has a greater expectation of help from his neighbor[2] than anyone else." Some said, "If a man wants to buy a house there is no harm done if he uses trickery to prevent another from buying it." Abu Abdullah said, "So that man says that some people are allowed to play tricks on other Muslims though Mohammed said, 'When doing business with other Muslims do not sell them sick animals or defective or stolen goods.'"

B8,73,70 Mohammed: "Harming a Muslim is an evil act; killing a Muslim means rejecting Allah."

A Muslim can swear a false oath by any other god and not be accountable.

B8,73,73 Mohammed: "A Muslim who swears a false oath by the god of another religion is not obligated to fulfill that promise because he cannot be bound by a faith he does not hold."

POSITION TOWARD OTHER RELIGIONS

Well before Mohammed, since the most ancient days, Mecca had been a center of religious tolerance. Many religions used Mecca as a pilgrim site. Mohammed's deathbed wishes were to create religious apartheid in Arabia and to use money to influence nonbelievers for Islam.

B4,52,288 "On his deathbed Mohammed gave three final orders saying, 'First, drive the non-Muslims from Arabia. Second, give gifts and show respect to foreign officials as I have done.' I forgot the third command."

---

1. Mohammed emigrated from Mecca to Medina. The Immigrant is a sacred figure in Islam.

2. Other hadiths show that neighbor meant other Muslims who lived in their own neighborhoods.

SECURITY

B1,8,386 Mohammed: "Whoever follows our prayer rituals and dietary commands is a Muslim and is protected by Allah and Mohammed. Do not betray those protected by Allah because, if you do, you also betray Allah."

This hadith details security, education, and slavery.

B4,53,397 Ali: "Muslims have no need to read anything other than the word of Allah and the legal regulations in this paper that govern the compensation for injuries, the condition of livestock used to pay taxes that support the needy, the payment of blood money, and the status of Medina as a sanctuary.

Therefore, anyone who sins against the doctrine, or falsely adds to it, or protects someone who does will be cursed by Allah, the people, and the angels. No amount of good acts will mitigate this transgression. Any freed slave who rejects the mastery of his former owner for the friendship of another will also be cursed. Protection granted by one Muslim must be upheld by all Muslims. Whoever violates the protection granted by a Muslim will also be cursed by Allah, the people, and the angels."

SLAVERY

The reason for the tax exemption on horses was jihad. Mohammed gave cavalrymen three times the amount he gave foot soldiers from the spoils of war (the wealth of the vanquished) to build a better cavalry.

B2,24,542 Mohammed: "Horses and slaves owned by a Muslim are tax exempt."

It is forbidden to capture a Muslim and make him a slave. If a slave converts to Islam, then there is a benefit in freeing him. But there is no benefit in freeing a non-Muslim slave. Islamic slavery is a blessing because sooner or later the slave or the slave's descendants will convert to Islam in order to be free.

B3,46,693 Mohammed said, "If a man frees a Muslim slave, Allah will free him from the fires of Hell in the same way that he freed the slave." Bin Marjana said that, after he related that revelation to Ali, the man freed a slave for whom he had been offered one thousand dinars by Abdullah.

JIHAD

CHAPTER 27

*61:11 Believe in Allah and His messenger and fight valiantly
for Allah's cause [jihad] with both your wealth and your
lives. It would be better for you, if you only knew it!*

The ethical system of the Hadith prepares the foundation of jihad. There is one set of ethics for the Muslim and another set of ethics for the non-Muslim (*kafir*). There are two ways to deal with non-Muslims. One is to treat them as inferiors but in a kindly way. The other is jihad.

Jihad is a unique word. Its actual meaning is struggle or effort. Islam talks of two kinds—the lesser jihad and the greater jihad. The greater jihad is spiritual effort or internal struggle, to stop smoking, for example, or control one's greed. Only three percent of the hadiths Bukhari recorded about jihad refer to the greater jihad.

The lesser jihad, armed struggle, is usually called "holy war," but this term is simplistic and far too narrow. It means, in fact, fighting in the cause of Allah, and it encompasses an entire way of life.

The dual ethics are established by the sacred texts of Islam—treating Muslims one way and non-Muslims another—are the basis of jihad. Perhaps the clearest expression of this duality is a phrase known to all Muslims: The world is divided into—

dar al Islam, land of submission, and

dar al harb, land of war.

The land of war is the country that is free of Islam, free of Allah. The land of the non-Muslim must become the land of those who have submitted and are the slaves of Allah. The Trilogy repeatedly stresses that Islam should be in a state of constant pressure against unbelievers; therefore, the relation between Islam and the rest of the world is sacred war or temporary peace. This struggle is eternal, universal, and obligatory for all Muslims. The only pause in jihad comes through the need for Islam to strengthen itself. Peace is temporary. War is permanent.

Jihad is laid out in all three of the Trilogy texts.

THE FUNDAMENTALS OF JIHAD

Political Islam is universal and eternal.

M001,0031 Mohammed: "I have been ordered to wage war against mankind until they accept that there is no god but Allah and that they believe I am His prophet and accept all revelations spoken through me. When they do these things I will protect their lives and property unless otherwise justified by Islamic law, in which case their fate lies in Allah's hands."

OBLIGATION

All Muslims have an obligation to perform jihad. Jihad is second only to prayer and respect for one's parents.

B1,10,505 Abdullah asked Mohammed, "What act is most beloved by Allah?" Mohammed answered, "To pray at the specified times." Abdullah then asked, "What is the next highest good?" He said, "Honor and obey your parents." I asked a third time, "What is the next highest good?" Mohammed replied, "To wage holy war in the name of Allah." Abdullah concluded, "I did not ask the next highest good, but if I had, Mohammed would have told me."

Jihad is one of the best actions that a Muslim can perform.

B2,26,594 Someone asked Mohammed, "What is the greatest act a Muslim can perform?" He said, "Accept Allah as the only god and that I am His prophet." Mohammed was then asked, "What is the next best act?" He answered, "To wage holy war in the name of Allah." Mohammed was then asked, "What is the next highest good?" He replied, "To make the sacred pilgrimage."

To commit suicide is a sure path to Hell. But to kill oneself in jihad is a sure path to eternal pleasure in Paradise.

B5,59,509 The army was arranged in rows at the battle at Khaybar. Amir's sword was short, and he aimed at the knee of a Jew. The sharp blade glanced off the Jew's knee and cut Amir's leg. He bled to death. After the battle, Al Akwa was sad and Mohammed asked him, "What is bothering you?" Al Akwa said, "They say Amir is lost because he killed himself." Mohammed said, "No, they are wrong. Amir will get a double reward [an elevated place in Paradise]." Mohammed raised two fingers. "Amir was a strong fighter in the Cause of Allah. There are few who have achieved such goodness as Amir."

The best Muslim is a jihadist. A saintly man is second best.

M020,4655 Mohammed: "The Muslim who lives the best life is the man who is always prepared to wage holy war in the name of Allah and who is constantly alert for the sound of war or a cry for help and always willing to face certain death. The next most virtuous life for a Muslim is the hermit who abides on a mountain or valley tending his herd, praying regularly, giving zakat [charity tax to be spent on Muslims], and worshiping Allah until he dies. There are no better men than these."

To avoid jihad is a great sin. The jihadist must be unafraid of death and never retreat except as a strategy. The enemy, the nonbeliever, must never be given mercy.

B4,51,28: Mohammed commanded, "Shun the seven deadly sins." Asked to elaborate, Mohammed said, "Worshiping gods other than Allah, witchcraft, the unsanctified murder of a believer, lending money at excessive rates of interest, squandering the assets of a ward or orphan, granting mercy to or fleeing from an unbelieving enemy in battle, and impugning the character of true believing, pure, and virginal women."

To be a real Muslim, one must aspire to be a jihadist.

M020,4696 Mohammed: "The man who dies without participating in jihad, who never desired to wage holy war, dies the death of a hypocrite."

Here we have prophetic hadiths. Jihad will be practiced into the future.

B4,152,146 Mohammed: "A time will come when the people will wage holy war, and it will be asked, 'Is there any amongst you who has enjoyed the company of Mohammed?' They will say: 'Yes.' And then victory will be bestowed upon them. They will wage holy war again, and it will be asked: 'Is there any among you who has enjoyed the company of the companions of Mohammed?' They will say: 'Yes.' And then victory will be bestowed on them."

M020,4712 Mohammed: "You shall conquer many lands and Allah will grant you victory over your enemies in battle, but none of you should stop practicing for war."

Fighting in jihad is demanded for all Muslims except for the frail or the crippled. To sit at home is inferior to jihad. Jihad is an obligation for all times and all places and for all Muslims.

B6,60,118 After the following verse was revealed to Mohammed, he called for a scribe,

> *"Not equal are those believers who sit at home and those who strive and fight in the Cause of Allah."*

After the scribe arrived with his writing utensils, Mohammed dictated his revelation. Ibn Um Maktum, who was present, exclaimed, "O Mohammed! But I am blind." A new revelation was then revealed that said:

> 4:95 *Believers who stay at home in safety, other than those who are disabled, are not equal to those who fight with their wealth and their lives for Allah's cause [jihad].*

Muslims should dedicate their jihad to their parents.

B8,73,3 A man once asked Mohammed, "Should I join the holy war?" Mohammed responded by asking if the man's parents were alive. When the man affirmed that they were, Mohammed answered, "Join the struggle for their sake."

Jihad is one of the highest goals of Islam, equal to charity and prayer.

B8,73,35 Mohammed: "The Muslim who does charitable works for the poor or elderly is like a holy warrior or a devout person who fasts all day and prays all night."

When the leader calls for jihad, every Muslim should take part immediately.

B4,52,42 Mohammed: "After the conquest of Mecca, there is no need to migrate to Medina, but holy war and the willingness to participate still remain. If your ruler demands warriors, answer his call immediately."

Here is Allah's contract with all Islam: to die in jihad is the sure way to go to Paradise. If the jihadist does not die, then he can keep what wealth he takes with violence from the enemy, the non-Muslim.

B4,52,46 Mohammed: "A Muslim holy warrior, fighting for Allah's cause is like a person who does nothing but fast and pray. Allah promises that anyone killed while fighting for His cause will be admitted without question into Paradise. If such a holy warrior survives the battles, he can return home with the captured property and possessions of the defeated."

A jihadist fights so that Islam will triumph, not just for wealth or fame. The jihadist is the purest and best Muslim.

B4,52,65 A man asked Mohammed, "One man fights for wealth, one man fights to achieve fame, and another fights for pride. Who among them fights for the cause of Allah?" Mohammed said, "The man who fights so that Islam should dominate is the man who fights for Allah's cause."

B4,52,72 Mohammed: "After entering Paradise no one would want to return to the world even though he might have everything in it, the only exception being the Muslim warrior who would return to be martyred ten times more for the honor he received from Allah."

All the non-Muslims who fight against jihad are doomed to burn in Hell for defending their culture and civilization.

B4,52,72 Mohammed told us that Allah revealed to him that "any holy warrior killed will go to Paradise." Umar asked the prophet, "Is it true that Muslims killed in battle will go to Paradise and non-Muslims who are killed in battle will go to Hell?" Mohammed said, "Yes."

A Muslim should support jihadists in every way. This includes financing the fighters and supporting their families.

B4,52,96 Mohammed: "Anyone who arms a jihadist is rewarded just as a fighter would be; anyone who gives proper care to a holy warrior's dependents is rewarded just as a fighter would be."

The smallest detail of supporting jihad brings a great reward.

B4,52,105 Mohammed: "If a man, motivated by belief in Allah and the promises Allah makes, gives a horse to be used for jihad, he will be rewarded on Judgment Day for the food and water the horse consumed and the waste it expelled."

Practicing jihad for even one day puts a believer in Paradise and is better than all the world.

B4,52,142 Mohammed: "To battle non-Muslims in jihad for even one day is greater than the entire earth and everything on it. A spot in Paradise smaller than your riding crop is greater than the entire earth and everything on it. A day or a night's travel in jihad is greater than the entire world and everything on it."

M020,4645 Mohammed said: "Abu Sa'id, anybody that happily acclaims Allah as his God, Islam as his faith, and Mohammed as his prophet must be admitted into Paradise." Abu Sa'id marveled at this and said, "Mohammed, say that again." Mohammed repeated his statement and added, "Another act raises a man's status in Paradise a hundred-fold; the difference between one level and another is equivalent to the distance between the heavens and the earth." Abu Sa'id asked, "What is this act?" Mohammed said, "Wage war for Allah! Wage war for Allah!"

Jihad cannot stop until all of the world has submitted to Islam. All non-believers' lives and wealth can and will be taken by jihad. Only those who submit to Islam will be spared.

B4,52,196 Mohammed: "I have been directed to fight the non-Muslim until every one of them admits, 'There is only one god and that is

Allah.' Whoever says, 'There is only one god and that is Allah,' his body and possessions will be protected by me except for violations of Islamic law, in which case his fate is with Allah, to be punished or forgiven, as He sees fit."

One of the first things Mohammed taught new Muslims was the distribution of the spoils of war.

B4,53,327 A delegation came to Mohammed from Rabia and asked the prophet for instructions for their tribe. Mohammed said, "I command you to perform five actions and I forbid you to do one act: accept Allah as the only god, perform your prayers strictly according to ritual, pay the charitable tax [*zakat*] for the support of the needy, fast during the month of Ramadan, give twenty percent of the property looted from non-Muslims to Allah, and never drink alcohol."

INVESTMENT OF MONEY IN JIHAD

Allah rewards those who give to jihad and curses those who do not.

B2,24,522 Mohammed: "Two angels descend from Paradise each day. One says, 'O, Allah! Reward those who contribute to jihad,' and the other says, 'O, Allah! Kill those who refuse to support jihad.'"

Jihad is supported by the Islamic tax structure and can make a man rich.

B2,24,547 A man ordered by Mohammed to collect a duty supporting jihad returned to him and reported that Ibn Jamil, Khalid, and Abbas refused to pay the tax. Mohammed asked, "Ibn Jamil was a poor man made rich by Allah and me. What makes him think he can refuse to pay his tax? It is unfair to ask Khalid to pay the tax because he remains a holy warrior for Allah. Abbas, however, is my uncle and the tax is mandatory for him. In fact, he should pay twice the amount."

Allah says a Muslim should spend his money on jihad.

B6,60,41 Hudhaifa said, "The following verse was revealed to Mohammed regarding the financial support of jihad."

> 2:195 *Spend your wealth generously for Allah's cause [jihad] and do not use your own hands to contribute to your destruction. Do good, for surely Allah loves those that do good.*

B8,78,633 I [Abu Dhar] joined Mohammed as he was sitting in the shade of the Kabah. He kept repeating, "They are the losers, by Allah! They are the losers!" I fretted to myself, "What have I done wrong? Does he perceive something improper in me?" As I sat beside him, Mohammed kept repeating, "They are the losers." Allah knows how anxious I was. I could not remain silent. I asked him, "Who are the losers? I would sacrifice my parents for you, Mohammed." He said, "The losers are the rich, except those who give money for jihad."

B4,52,94 Mohammed said, "Whoever spends even a small amount on jihad will be welcomed by name by the gate-keepers of Paradise."

Abu Bakr said, "O, Mohammed! People like that will never be destroyed."

Mohammed said, "It is my wish that you will be such a person."

M020,4668 Mohammed: "A person who financially supports a fighter for jihad is morally equivalent to an actual fighter. A person who cares for a warrior's family during his service is morally equivalent to an actual fighter."

The wealth of Islam comes from jihad.

B4,53,350 Mohammed: "When the Persian king is destroyed, his line will end with him. When Caesar is destroyed, there will be no more Caesars. By Him who holds my life in His hands, you will spend his wealth in jihad against the rest of the world."

GOALS

The goal of jihad is the dominance of Islam over all other political systems and religions.

B1,3,125 A man asked Mohammed, "Mohammed, what manner of fighting can be considered done for the sake of Allah? Some fight because they are angry and some for their pride." Mohammed looked up at the man and said, "The man who fights to make Islam dominant is the man who fights for Allah's cause."

All other religions must submit to Islam. Then and only then will jihad stop. Until that time no person, other than a Muslim, is safe.

B1,8,387 Mohammed said, "I have been commanded to fight the non-Muslims until they admit: 'There is one god and He is Allah.' If they admit this, pray as we do, face Mecca as we do, and prepare their meat as we do, then their persons and possessions will be sacred to us and we will not limit them except in legal matters. Their judgment rests with Allah."

"Abu Hamza, what makes a person's life or possessions sacred?"

He [Abu Hamza] answered, "If a person gives witness that there is but one god, Allah, and if he prays like we do and faces Mecca, and if he obeys our dietary commands, then he is a Muslim and has the same entitlements and obligations as the rest of us. These things make a person's body and possessions sacred."

When jihad is successful, it is not the Muslim who is successful but Allah. Jihad is the triumph of Allah over the non-Muslim.

B3,27,23 Whenever Mohammed returned from a Holy Battle, or pilgrimage, he used to say, "Allah is great," three times. Every time Mohammed returned from jihad or Hajj, he would exclaim at every hill three times, "God is great," and then he would say, "There is no god but Allah; He is perfect and has no partners. He reigns over all kingdoms and all praise is due him. He is all-powerful. We return filled with repentance: praying, bowing down, and giving praise. Allah honored His promise and gave victory to His slave. Allah alone subjugated the non-Muslims."

REWARDS

A Muslim martyr is one who kills for Allah and Islam. But his killing must be pure and devoted only to Allah. If his motivation is pure, then the jihadist will achieve Paradise or be able to take the wealth of the nonbeliever.

B1,2,35 Mohammed said, "The man who joins jihad, compelled by nothing except sincere belief in Allah and His Prophets, and survives, will be rewarded by Allah either in the afterlife or with the spoils of war. If he is killed in battle and dies a martyr, he will be admitted into Paradise. Were it not for the difficulties it would cause my followers, I would never stay behind while my soldiers head off for jihad. If I could, I would love to be martyred in jihad, be resurrected, and martyred again and again for Allah."

No matter what sins a jihadist commits, he will not go to Hell.

B2,13,30 I [Abu Abs] heard Mohammed say, "Anyone who even gets his feet dirty performing jihad will be saved from Hell by Allah."

The pure jihadist must commit his life and wealth to jihad. If he can reach this highest form of devotion, then not even the pilgrimage to Mecca (the Hajj) can surpass it.

B2,15,86 Mohammed said, "No good act during the rest of the year is better than departing on Hajj." Some of his companions asked, "What about jihad?" Mohammed answered, "Even jihad is inferior unless a man knowingly risks and loses both life and property for the sake of Allah."

M020,4649 Mohammed: "Except debt, all sins of a martyr are forgiven."

B3,31,121 Mohammed said, "Anyone who gives more than his share to support the cost of jihad will be called and greeted at the gates of Paradise with, 'O slave of Allah! Here is wealth.' Anyone who scrupulously prayed will be called into Paradise from the gate of prayer; anyone who joined jihad will be called from the gate of jihad; anyone who fasted correctly will be called to the gate of fulfillment; anyone who gave alms will be called from the gate of charity." Abu Bakr said, "I would sacrifice my parents for you Mohammed! Nothing bad will happen to those called from those gates. Will anyone be called from all of them?" Mohammed answered, "Yes, I hope that you are one."

Paradise lies in the shade of swords.

M020,4681 Mohammed said, "Certainly, the gates of Paradise lie in the shade of swords." A shabby man rose and asked Abu Musa if he had heard Mohammed say this. "Yes," he replied. The shabby man then rejoined his friends and said his good-byes. He then unsheathed his sword, broke and discarded its scabbard, advanced upon the enemy, and fought until he was killed.

M020,4694 Mohammed: "A man who sincerely pursues martyrdom, even if he is not killed, shall still receive its reward."

After jihad, Ali had the money necessary for the obligatory marriage dowry.

B3,34,302 As my [Ali's] share of the spoils of war I received an old she-camel, and Mohammed gave me another from his share. When my marriage to Fatima [Mohammed's daughter] approached, I hired a Jewish goldsmith to assist me in bringing a load of ldhkhir grass for resale to other goldsmiths, the proceeds to pay for my wedding reception.

A jihadist can benefit Islam and achieve personal gain.

B3,34,313 We departed with Mohammed in the year of the battle of Hunain. Mohammed gave me a captured suit of armor which I sold. I [Abu Qatada] took the money from the armor and bought a garden near the Bani Salama tribe. That was the first property I received after converting to Islam.

Mohammed became rich from jihad, so rich that he could pay the debts of dead jihadists.

B3,37,495 Every time a Muslim died in debt and was brought to Mohammed he asked, "Has he any property to repay his debts?" If the dead man had assets, then Mohammed would offer the funeral prayers. If not, he told the man's friends to offer the funeral prayer. After Allah made

Mohammed rich by conquering the non-Muslims, he said, "I have a greater obligation than other Muslims to be the guardian of Islam; therefore if a Muslim dies in debt, I am responsible for settling that debt. If a Muslim dies leaving assets and no debt, then it will belong to his heirs."

B3,47,757 After a delegation from the Hawazin met with Mohammed, the prophet addressed the people, gave deserved thanks and praise to Allah, and said, "Your brothers have come begging forgiveness and freedom for their captured tribe members. I think it is reasonable that we grant it. If any of you will meet my request, I'll consider it a favor. If you choose to keep your share of the spoils of war until the next victory, then you will be reimbursed at that time." The audience responded, "As a favor to you, we will free those slaves."

Mohammed used the spoils of war as a reward for those who were new to Islam. Money is one of the ways to influence those who are weak in Islam.

B4,53,373 Mohammed gave gifts to some and to others he did not. Those who did not receive gifts felt slighted and complained. Mohammed said, "I give presents to some people so that they do not stray from the path, or become disenchanted. Others simply need to be reminded of the wonder and pleasure Allah gives them. Amr is such a person." Amr said, "The words of the prophet are more valuable to me than red camels."

War treasure was a routine source of income to the jihadists.

B3,35,456 Abu Burda and Abdullah delegated me [Bin Abi] to inquire about rules governing the immediate payment for goods. They said, "When we accompanied Mohammed, we received spoils of war. We would pay the peasants of Sham in advance for goods and materials that would be delivered by a certain time." I asked, "Did the peasants own and maintain crop land for cultivation?" They answered, "We never asked."

Mohammed often used money to influence others about Islam.

B4,53,374 Mohammed: "I give money to the Quraysh to tempt them into remaining true to Islam, because they are new to the faith and their lives of ignorance are a short distance away."

To die in jihad is the best life.

B5,59,377 During the battle of Uhud, a man asked Mohammed, "Where will I go if I am killed in battle?" Mohammed said, "Paradise." The man then threw away the meal that he was carrying, joined the battle, and fought until he was killed.

Jihad is an obligation, not a recommendation. Allah demands jihad, now and forever, from all Muslims in all places and for all times.

B5,59,379 When the Koran was being compiled, I [Zaid] overlooked a verse that I had heard Mohammed recite. It was found after some searching. The verse read:

> 33:23 *Some among the believers have been faithful in their covenant with Allah. Some of them have fulfilled their covenant with their deaths, and some are waiting for death, and they have not wavered in their determination.*

We then added the verse to the Koran.

Although Muslims can get to Paradise without jihad, jihadists will dwell in the highest levels there. Those who do not enter jihad must be judged on the Final Day. Their outcome is uncertain and they will suffer punishment of the grave. The jihadist goes straight to Paradise without judgment or suffering.

B4,52,48 Mohammed said, "Allah will accept anyone into Paradise who accepts Allah as the one god and Mohammed as His prophet, prays strictly according to ritual, and fasts during Ramadan, even if he didn't fight jihad or make a pilgrimage." The people asked, "Shall we tell the people the good news?" Mohammed said, "There are one hundred levels in Paradise reserved for jihadis who fight for Allah. The difference between one level and the next is comparable to the distance between Heaven and Earth. Therefore, when you request something from Allah, request the highest level of Paradise."

The very best of rewards awaits the martyrs of jihad.

B4,52,49 Mohammed said, "I dreamt last night that two men forced me to climb a tree whereupon I was taken into a wonderful house, the like of which I have never seen. One man said, 'This is the house of martyrs.'"

One fight in Allah's Cause is better than the rewards of the entire world.

B4,52,53 Mohammed: "Nobody who died and went to Paradise would want to return to life even if he were given the world and all its possessions, the exception being the martyr who recognized the moral superiority of giving his life for Allah and who wished to return to life only to give it again. A single act of jihad in the afternoon or morning is greater than the entire world and everything in it. A place in Paradise, no matter how small, is greater than the entire world and everything in it. If a houri [a virgin of Paradise devoted to perfect sexual satisfaction] came from Paradise and revealed herself to man, she would fill the sky between heaven and earth with bright light and sweet aromas. The veil she wears is greater than the entire earth and everything in it."

No matter how little a Muslim does, if he dies in jihad, he will be given the highest rewards. Good works and morality pale in comparison to the rewards of jihad.

B4,52,63 A man, his face shielded by his helmet, asked Mohammed, "Should I join the battle or accept Islam first?" Mohammed answered, "Accept Allah and then join the fight." The man accepted Islam and was killed shortly after. Mohammed said, "A small effort but a great prize. Even though he did not do much after accepting Islam, he shall be richly rewarded."

Mohammed was the perfect jihadist, and those who remember him (imitate him) will be given victory by Allah.

B4,52,146 Mohammed: "There will come a time when men leaving for jihad will be asked, 'Did any of you fight alongside Mohammed?' They will answer, 'Yes.' Allah will then grant them victory over the non-Muslim. Later there will come a time when men leaving for jihad will be asked, 'Did any of you fight alongside the men who fought alongside Mohammed?' They will answer, 'Yes,' and Allah will grant them victory. Then there will come a time when people will ask, 'Did any of you fight alongside the men who fought alongside the men who fought alongside Mohammed?' They will answer, 'Yes,' and victory will be granted them also."

Slaves were a part of jihad.

B4,53,344 When Fatima, Mohammed's daughter, received word that Mohammed had been given a number of slave girls as his share of spoils of war, she hoped that her strains from manual labor might be relieved. When she could not find Mohammed, Fatima told Aisha, Mohammed's favorite wife, that she wished to have a maid. Aisha passed her request to Mohammed, who visited the women after they had gone to bed. When they arose to greet him, Mohammed said, "Stay where you are." Mohammed put his foot on Fatima's chest and said, "Do you want to know what is better than a maid? Before going to bed, say, 'Allah is Great,' thirty-four times. Say, 'All praise to Allah,' thirty-three times, and say, 'Glory to Allah,' thirty-three times. This is better than asking for a maid."

Enslavement of the nonbelievers and theft of their property were made sacred for Mohammed. Since Mohammed is the ideal pattern of behavior for all Muslims at all times and all places, the wealth of nonbelievers is meant to be taken by others in Islam.

B4,53,351 Mohammed: "Allah has made it legal for me to take spoils of war."

Allah has a contractual agreement with all jihadists. If they die in jihad, Allah will reward them above all people. If they don't die, then they can profit by theft. So the jihadist has guarantees of profit in both this world and the next.

B4,53,352 Mohammed: "Allah promises the jihadi with pure intent either a place in Paradise or a return to his home with spoils of war and the guarantee of Allah's reward in the afterlife."

The wealth of Islam comes from what is taken from the nonbelievers after jihad.

B4,53,358 During the battle of Al-Jamal, Az-Zubair looked over the battle field, called me [Abdulla, his son] to him and said as we stood there, "My son, people are going to be killed today. Some will be oppressors, some will be oppressed. I will be killed as an oppressed one. My greatest concern is my debts. Do you believe that we will have any money left after paying off all my notes?" He then added, "Son, sell our assets and settle my debts."

Although Az-Zubair never held a lucrative post, he saved his shares of spoils of war that had been allotted to him during battles alongside Mohammed, Abu Bakr, Umar, and Uthman....Anxious to gain their father's wealth, Az-Zubair's sons said, "Give us our inheritance now." Az-Zubair said, "No, by Allah. You won't get your inheritance until I have announced at four consecutive pilgrimages a call for anyone with money claims against me to come and allow me to settle the debt." After four years of doing so, Az-Zubair distributed his estate among his sons and his four wives. The value of the estate was 50,200,000 dinars [a fortune from the spoils of war of jihad].

SEX

Forced sex with the female captives of jihad was standard practice for Mohammed and his companions. These captives became slaves used for sex, and Mohammed had his choice of the most attractive new slaves. This is the ideal pattern of Islam.

B3,34,431 One of the captives was a beautiful Jewess, Safiya. Dihya had her first, but she was given to Mohammed next.

Mohammed accepted the forced sex with non-Muslims.

B3,34,432 While sitting with Mohammed, I [Abu Said Al-Khudri] asked, "Mohammed, sometimes we receive female slaves as our share of the spoils. Naturally, we are concerned about their retaining their value [the sex slaves were worth less money if they were pregnant when sold]. How do you feel about *coitus interruptus?*" Mohammed asked, "Do you do that? It is better not to do that. It is Allah's will whether or not a child is born."

Mohammed did not discourage forced sex but said if Allah wanted the slaves to be pregnant then nothing could prevent it. There are many prohibitions about sex in Islam, but none of them applies to sex with slaves.

B9,93,506 The Muslims captured some females during the battle of Bani Al-Mustaliq and planned to rape them but did not want them impregnated. They asked Mohammed if there were any restrictions against *coitus interruptus.* Mohammed told them that it was better that they should not interrupt their ejaculation. "It is preferable that you not do it because Allah has already determined everyone who will be born until the end of time." Mohammed said, "No life will be created if Allah does not create it."

M008,3432 After the battle of Hunain, Mohammed attacked Autas. The companions of Mohammed achieved victory and took many captives, including many women, and they were reluctant to have sex with the captive women because their husbands were polytheists and held as captives nearby. Allah then revealed to Mohammed,

> 4:24 *You are also forbidden to marry two sisters at the same time, with the exception of those whom you have already married [married before the Koran]. Truly Allah is forgiving and merciful! Also forbidden to you are married women unless they are your slaves. This is the command of Allah. Other than those mentioned, all other women are lawful to you to court with your wealth and with honorable intentions, not with lust. And give those you have slept with a dowry, as it is your duty. But after you have fulfilled your duty, it is not an offense to make additional agreements among you. Truly Allah is knowing and wise! [emphasis added]*

BATTLES

In his last nine years Mohammed was involved in sixty-five events of violence, an average of one violent event every seven weeks. This total does not include acts of summary execution and assassinations.

The Jews of Khaybar were warned that they had been called to submit to Islam. They refused, and they were destroyed and made dhimmis (semi-slaves).

B5,59,285 Once, Zaid and I [Abu Ishaq] were sitting together, and someone asked him, "How many battles did Mohammed wage for Allah?" Zaid replied, "Nineteen." He was then asked, "How many battles did you fight alongside the Prophet?" He answered, "Seventeen." I asked him, "What was the first battle you fought alongside Mohammed?" Zaid said, "Al-Ashira or Al-Ashiru."

B1,11,584 When Mohammed led us into battle, he did not let us attack at night; instead he had us wait until morning. If morning prayers were heard he would delay the assault, and if the prayers were not heard, then the attack would commence.

After reaching Khaybar during the night we waited until morning to hear if they called to prayer. When the call was not heard, we rode into battle with Abi Talha ahead and Mohammed and me side by side.

The people of Khaybar were emerging from the town carrying their tools when they saw us. They screamed, "Mohammed! Oh my god, Mohammed's army!" Mohammed saw them and said, "Allah is great! Allah is great! Khaybar is destroyed." When we rode against a non-Muslim country, those people whom we had warned were in for an evil morning.

Jihad is a sacred act, and it should not interfere with prayer. But war demands practicality, so the jihadist should practice Islam so that it does not endanger the goals of jihad.

B2,14,65 Ibn Umar:

When Muslims and non-Muslims face each other in battle, Muslims may pray without prostrating themselves. Ibn Umar added, "Mohammed said, 'If the enemy outnumbers our forces, the Muslim soldier may pray while standing or riding a mount.'"

Safiya was the most beautiful of the Jews. Mohammed assassinated her husband, killed her cousins, and tortured her father to death.

B2,14,68 During the night Mohammed said the Fajr prayer, mounted his beast and said, "God is great! Khaybar is destroyed! When we ride against a nation that has ignored our warning, they are in for the most terrible morning." As the people emerged from the city and saw our forces, they screamed the warning, "Mohammed and his army are here." Mohammed crushed them, killing their warriors and seizing their women and children. Dihya Al-Kalbi took Safiya, although she was later given to Mohammed, who married her and gave her her freedom as a wedding present.

Jihadists do not fear death and are brave.

B2,23,338 Mohammed said, "Zaid was our flag bearer and was killed. Jafar took the flag and was also killed. Abdullah then took the flag, but he was killed also," and Mohammed's eyes filled with tears. "Khalid then took the flag, though he was not yet a chief, and Allah blessed him with victory."

Though Mohammed would mourn the death of Muslims, there is not a recorded event where he expressed any regret or remorse at the death and suffering of any non-Muslim opponent.

B2,23,387 I never saw Mohammed sadder than he was the day that the reciters of the Koran [men who had memorized the Koran] were killed. He prayed for an entire month for the destruction of his enemies.

B2,23,452 After the battle of Badr, the bodies of the non-Muslims were thrown in a well where Mohammed addressed them, "Do you still believe the promises of your god?" Somebody said, "You are talking to dead people." Mohammed answered, "They hear as well as you, but they can't talk back."

Mecca had been a town of sanctuary before Islam, and Ibn Khatal was there seeking refuge as an apostate.

B3,29,72 When Mohammed entered Mecca after its fall to the Muslims, he removed the Arabian helmet he was wearing, signaling the end of the battle. Someone came to him and said, "Ibn Khatal has sought refuge in the Kabah." Mohammed said, "Kill him."

The Jews were date farmers. One of the tactics of jihad is to attack economic assets [this was a goal of September 11, 2001 attack].

B3,39,519 Mohammed destroyed the date orchards of the Jews and Hassan wrote this poetic verse: "The chiefs of Bani LuAi enjoyed watching the Jew's trees consumed by fire."

B3,48,832 The night before the battle of Uhud, Mohammed ordered me to present myself before him. I was fourteen at the time, and he did not allow me to fight in that battle. I was fifteen when he called me before him on the eve of the battle of the Trench, and he gave his permission for me to fight. Nafi' said, "I told this story to Umar, who was caliph at the time, and he said, 'Fifteen is the boundary between boyhood and manhood.' He then wrote his governors telling them to pay salaries to jihadists when they reach fifteen.

All of the earth is the domain of Islam, and all of the wealth of the world belongs to Islam. The only safety from jihad is to become a Muslim.

B4,53,392 Leaving the Mosque one day Mohammed said, "Let's go speak to the Jews." When we arrived Mohammed said, "You will be safe if you accept Islam. The earth belongs to Allah and myself, and I want you out of here. If you own any property, you may sell it, but you need to know that the world belongs to Allah and Mohammed."

It is a duty to kill those who resist Islam. Killing in jihad is a blessing.

B5,58,160 Before Islam became supreme, there was a house called Dhul-Khalasa. Mohammed asked me, "Will you take care of Dhul-Khalasa for me?" I took one hundred and fifty riders with me and destroyed the house and killed everyone we found. When we returned and reported back to Mohammed, he called upon Allah to bless us.

It is the will of Allah that Islam should triumph in jihad.

B5,59,289 Before the battle of Badr, Mohammed prayed, "Allah, I beseech you to honor your promise and agreement with us. If you desire that no one worship you, then let the non-Muslims triumph." Abu Bakr then took him by his hand and said, "You have done enough." Mohammed then said,

54:45 *They will be routed and will turn their backs and run.*

Violence determines truth in Islam.

B5,59,316 Aisha says this quote was attributed by Ibn Umar to Mohammed: "The dead are punished because of the grieving of their families." Aisha, however, said, "But Mohammed said, 'The dead are punished for their transgressions while their families grieve.'" She also said, "This is much like the words spoken by Mohammed to the corpses in the well at Badr, 'They hear my words.'" And she said, "He said, 'Now they know that I was telling the truth.'"

No amount of suffering will discourage the jihadists.

B8,76,460 Sa'd was the first Arab to wage jihad. He said, "At times during jihad, there was nothing to eat except the leaves of desert trees. Our waste resembled that of a sheep. Nowadays, the Bani Asad instruct me in the rules of Islam. If I have to listen to them, I am done for, and all of my suffering has been wasted."

This next hadith is of great importance. Amir killed himself while trying to kill non-Muslims during jihad. Suicide is a crime against Allah and a sentence to Hell. His fellow jihadists said that since he had killed himself he was lost. Mohammed said that killing oneself in jihad is not suicide and instead earns the jihadist the highest reward.

Non-Muslims today call such jihadists "suicide bombers" but that is not accurate. The formal name for those who try to commit suicide in the name of jihad is *mujahadeen* and for those who succeed it is *shaeen*.

Some Muslims claim that since suicide is against Islam the human bombers are not Islamic. That statement is an example of *taqiyya* (sacred deceit).

Suicide is a sin in Islam, but killing oneself in jihad is not considered suicide; it is actually the highest form of Islam.

B9,83,29 Our company was traveling to Khaybar with Mohammed when someone called out, "Amir, sing some of your camel-driving songs." He complied, singing several songs whose rhythm mimicked the gait of camels. Mohammed was pleased and asked, "Who is that man?" "Amir," someone told him. Mohammed then said, "May Allah show mercy to him." Several of us said, "Mohammed, we hope that you will let him stay with us for a while," but he was killed early the next day.

We were very upset. Several people remarked, "It is too bad that all of Amir's good deeds have gone to waste, because he is damned for killing himself." When I heard those remarks, I went to Mohammed and said, "Prophet of Allah, I would sacrifice my father for you, but the people say that Amir is damned." Mohammed said, "Then those people lie. Amir will be doubly rewarded because he strove to be obedient to Allah, and he fought in jihad. No other death would bring so great a reward."

In the hour of final judgment by Allah, those killed by jihad will find that death was small compared to eternal punishment for resisting Islam. First, the jihadist causes suffering and death; then Allah causes suffering for eternity.

B4,52,164 Mohammed sat in his tent shortly before the battle of Badr and said, "Allah, I beg you to honor our contract and your promise. If you wish our destruction, you will never be worshiped again." Abu Bakr grabbed his hand and said, "That will do, Mohammed! You have vigorously pleaded with Allah." Mohammed, clad in armor, went out and said to me:

54:45 *They will be routed and will turn their backs and run. No! The Hour of Judgment is their promised time, and that hour will be terrible and bitter.*

Khalid confirms that this occurred at the battle of Badr.

Mohammed used deception with his enemies.

B4,52,198 When Mohammed planned an attack, he would use deceit to conceal his objective. (Ka'b would say, "Mohammed rarely began an attack on any day but Thursday.") The exception being the battle of Tabuk which was fought during extremely hot weather. Facing a long trek through the desert before attacking a formidable host, Mohammed told his army their destination and made clear their difficult situation.

Allegiance to Islam is allegiance to death.

B4,52,207 I [Salama] promised loyalty to Mohammed and then cooled myself in the shadow of a tree. As the crowd around Mohammed began to thin, he asked, "Ibn Al-Akwa! Will we do so again?" So I pledged my allegiance to him a second time. I asked, "Abu Muslim, what kind of pledge did you give Mohammed?" He answered, "I pledged my death."

In jihad, patience is a virtue.

B4,52,210 Once during battle, Mohammed spoke to the people as the sun was going down and said, "Do not willingly go into battle and beg Allah to protect you from harm. If you do go into battle, have patience and remember that Paradise lies in the shadow of swords." Mohammed then said, "Allah, bestower of the Koran, master of the elements, conqueror of the pagans, defeat the non-Muslim and give us victory."

A tactical mission.

B4,52,259 While giving orders for a mission he wished us to undertake, Mohammed said, "If you find so-and-so, burn them with fire." Just as we were leaving, however, Mohammed said, "Although I have ordered you to burn those two men, I realize only Allah may punish with fire, so if you do find them, just kill them."

Assassination is a tactic of jihad and was used frequently by Mohammed. Not one person in Arabia who opposed or criticized Mohammed lived except by fleeing or converting. Assassinations were common and feared.

B4,52,265 Mohammed ordered a band of Helpers to assassinate Abu Rafi. One of the group, Abdullah, slipped into his house at night and killed him in his sleep."

All nonbelievers who resist in any way can be killed as an act of jihad.

B4,52,286 Mohammed was traveling one time when a non-Muslim spy came to him. After sitting and talking a while with Mohammed and his companions, the spy departed. Mohammed said, "Chase him down and kill him." So, I [Al Akwa] did. Mohammed rewarded me with the spy's possessions and his share of the spoils.

The spoils of war.

B4,53,362 Abdullah Bin Umar was in a detachment sent by Mohammed to Najd. They captured a large number of camels. Each of them was given eleven or twelve as his share and given an extra camel as a bonus.

Captives could be killed or ransomed.

B4,53,367 Speaking about the captives from the battle of Badr, Mohammed said, "If Al-Mutim were alive and if he asked me to, I would have freed those people for his sake."

Abu Jahl spoke against Mohammed, so he was marked for killing. Only those who submit are safe.

B4,53,369 At the battle of Badr, I, Abdur-Rahman, stood in the front line between two young boys and wished that I had been the stronger man. One of them got my attention and said, "Uncle, do you know Abu Jahl?" I said, "Yes, why do you ask?" He replied, "People tell me he speaks ill of Mohammed. By Allah, if I see him, I will not break off my attack until one of us is dead."

I was shocked to hear this. Then the other boy said the same thing to me. Sometime later, I saw Abu Jahl, and I pointed him out to the boys, saying, "There is the man you seek." After ferociously attacking and killing him, the boys went to Mohammed and told him of Abu Jahl's death. Mohammed asked, "Who killed him?" They both truthfully said, "I have killed him." Mohammed asked, "Did you clean your swords?" After they answered, "No," Mohammed glanced at their swords and said, "Obviously, you both killed him, so his possessions will be divided between the two of you."

Treaties are a part of jihad. The treaty of Hudaibiya recognized Islam as a political power, but the protection it offered to the nonbelievers was voided after Mohammed became strong enough to crush his opponents. Treaties are an element of strategy for giving Islam time to gain strength. In the end only submission will stop jihad.

B4,53,406 While in Siffin, Sahl arose and scolded the people saying, "Brothers, accept blame. We stood alongside of Mohammed at Hudaibiya, we would have fought if we had been asked to." Then Umar came to Mohammed and questioned him, "Mohammed, are we not right and our enemies wrong?" "Yes," Mohammed said. Umar asked, "Do not our slain soldiers reside in Paradise while theirs burn in Hell?" Mohammed said, "Yes." Exasperated, Umar asked, "Then why should we accept a bad treaty that limits Islam? Will this treaty last until Allah judges between the believers and the non-believers?" Mohammed said, "Ibn Al-Khattab, I am the prophet of Allah. Allah will never diminish me."

Umar then went to Abu Bakr and repeated the concerns he expressed to Mohammed. Abu Bakr said to him, "Mohammed is the prophet of Allah and Allah will never diminish him." The Victory sura of the Koran was then revealed to Mohammed who recited it in its entirety to Umar. Umar then asked, "Mohammed, was the treaty of Hudaibiya really a victory for Islam?" Mohammed said, "Yes."

No death is too painful or fearful for the nonbeliever. Allah will be even more cruel in Hell for eternity.

B8,82,795 Mohammed punished the men of the Uraina tribe by cutting off their hands and feet and letting them bleed to death.

Jihad is obligatory for a Muslim. Jihad was not just for the days of Mohammed but forever. The only proper response to jihad is immediate obedience to the call and need.

B4,53,41 On the day Mecca fell, Mohammed said, "There is no longer a need to migrate, but the necessity for jihad remains and so does the need for pure intent. When you are called to jihad, you should come immediately."

Mohammed also said that day, "When Allah created the heavens and the earth, he made Mecca a sanctuary. Before me, fighting was forbidden here, and Allah has made it legal for me only for this time.

"By Allah's order Mecca is a sanctuary until Judgment day. Its weeds should not be chopped, its animals should not be hunted, its lost belongings should not be disturbed except by someone who will publicly seek its true owner, and its grass should not be plowed."

Hearing that, Al-Abbas said, "Mohammed, What about the Idhkhir? It is used by the people to build their homes and by the goldsmiths." Mohammed then said, "Idhkhir is the exception."

MISCELLANEOUS

M020,4711 Mohammed: "Be ready to meet them with as much strength as you can muster. Remember, power rests in archery. Remember, power rests in archery. Remember, power rests in archery."

B5,59,400 Pointing to his broken front tooth, Mohammed said, "Allah's rage is severe on those who harmed His apostle. Allah's rage is severe on the man slain by His apostle during jihad."

Here we see that Mohammed used propaganda as one of Islam's most valuable weapons of jihad. Allah supports propaganda and the debasement of non-Muslims.

B5,59,449 Mohammed said to Hassan, "Insult them [the non-Muslims] with your poetry and Gabriel will protect you."

M031,6074 Mohammed said, "Hassan B. Thibit, satirize and mock the non-Muslim; Gabriel is by your side." This hadith was narrated with the authority of Shu'ba and the same line of transmitters.

Since Allah is the prime mover of jihad and actively helps jihadists, a very few jihadists can overcome superior forces. No enemy is too large or too strong for Islam. It is predestined that all opposition will be crushed by jihad. Only the time is unknown, not the final outcome.

B6,60,176 When the verse, "If there are twenty steadfast amongst you Muslims, they will overcome two hundred non-Muslims," was revealed, it hurt the morale of the jihadists. A ten-to-one advantage was too much to fight against. When Allah reduced this demand by revealing to Mohammed:

> 8:66 *Allah has now lessened your burden because He knows that there is weakness in you. If there are among you a hundred men who will stand fast, they will overcome two hundred.*

Then their morale improved.

Islam must annihilate the ancient religions.

M031,6052 According to Jabir, before the Muslim conquest of Arabia, there was a temple named Dhu'l-Khalasash also called the northern Kabah, or the Yamanite Kabah. "Mohammed asked me, 'Will you take care of Dhu'l-Khalasah for me?' I agreed and led three hundred and fifty Ahmas cavalrymen on a mission to destroy the temple and kill everyone we could lay hands upon. We informed Mohammed of our success immediately upon our return, and he blessed us and the entire tribe of the Ahmazs."

Jihad is the only sure path to Paradise.

B9,93,549 Mohammed said, "Allah promises that the Muslim who participates in jihad with no compulsion, other than true faith and the desire to serve Allah, will either be admitted into Paradise, or sent home with Allah's reward or a share of the spoils of war."

The remark of five words, "this is enough for me," was a death sentence for an old man.

B2,19,173 Mohammed would prostrate himself on the ground while reciting the Koran at Mecca. His companions followed his example [their piety was evident by the dirt on their foreheads] except for an old man who merely touched a handful of dirt and pebbles to his head and said, "This is enough for me." Soon after, I saw that man killed for being a non-Muslim.

The poetry of this hadith is the most elegant expression of jihad.

B4,52,73 Mohammed: "Be aware that Paradise lies under the shadow of swords."

Jihad should be waged at the right time. Haste should never be a priority.

B4,52,86 Mohammed: "When you prepare to fight your enemy, take your time."

Mohammed was the perfect jihadist.

B4,52,216 Mohammed: "If I did not have to worry about my disciples, I would never stay behind while soldiers march off to war. However, I don't have the means to transport them and I hate to leave them behind. Obviously, if I could I would fight and die in jihad, be resurrected and be martyred again."

War is deceit and jihad is deceit. Lies and deceit are one of the chief weapons of jihad.

B4,52,267 Mohammed: "The Persian king shall be killed, and there will not be another. Caesar will certainly be destroyed, and there will not be another, and you will exhaust their riches supporting jihad. War is deceit."

The following hadith led to the Jewish-Arabian holocaust. The second rightly guided caliph, Umar, drove out every Jew and Christian from Arabia, based upon this hadith. The only Jews left behind were used for sexual slavery. To this day, church and synagogue are forbidden in Arabia—religious apartheid. The use of money to influence others for Islam was the other of two final commands.

B4,53,393 Bin Jubair overheard Ibn Abbas mourning, "Thursday! Oh, you remember what happened on Thursday." Ibn Abbas then wept till the earth was muddied with tears. I asked Ibn Abbas, "What is the significance of Thursday?" He said, "Mohammed was on his deathbed and he said, "Bring me something to write with so that I may leave you instructions to keep you on the right path after I die." Although it was improper to do so, those present argued amongst themselves in front of Mohammed. Some said, "What is his problem? Is he mad, or delirious?" Mohammed said, "Let me be. I am better off dying than listening to you."

Mohammed then gave three orders saying, "Drive all the non-Muslims from Arabia and give gifts and respect to all foreign representatives just like I used to do." The secondary narrator concluded, "Either Ibn Abbas did not mention the third command, or I forgot what he said."

Here is a summary of jihad by Ibn Taymiya, a famous Islamic scholar of the fourteenth century:[1]

> In ordering jihad Allah has said:
>
> 2:193 *Fight them until you are no longer persecuted and the religion of Allah reigns absolute*
>
> Allah has, in fact, repeated this obligation [to fight] and has glorified jihad in most of the Medinan Suras; he has stigmatized those who neglected to fight in jihad and treated them as hypocrites and cowards.
>
> It is impossible to count the number of times when jihad and its virtues are extolled in the Koran and the Sunna [Sira and Hadith]. Jihad is the best form of voluntary service that man consecrates to Allah.
>
> Therefore, since jihad is divinely instituted with its goal of religion reverting in its entirety to Allah [all religions must submit to Islam], and to make Allah's word triumph, whoever opposes the realization of this goal will be fought, according to the unanimous opinion of Muslims.
>
> Jews and Christians, as well as Zoroastrians (Magians, followers of the native religion of the Persians) must be fought until they embrace Islam or pay the jizya (submission tax of humiliation) without recriminations. Muslim legal experts do not agree on whether the jizya should be imposed on other categories of infidels or not; on the other hand, all consider that it should not be required of Arabs [hence they should convert to Islam or be killed or expelled].

1.   Bat Ye'or, *Islam and Dhimmitude* (Associated University Press, Cranbury, NJ, 2003), 44.

SHARIA LAW

CHAPTER 23

4:59 Believers! Obey Allah and obey His Messenger
and those among you with authority. If you have a
disagreement about anything, refer it to Allah and His
Messenger if you believe in Allah and the Last Day.
This is the best and fairest way to settle a dispute.

Islam is a complete political, cultural, legal, and religious system. Since the system comes from Allah, it is perfect and eternal. The political goal of Islam is for every constitution and every form of government to be replaced by the sacred form of government, the Sharia. All governments of the non-Muslims are offensive to Allah. They are man-made and, therefore, not divine. It is historically inevitable that they will be replaced by the Sharia; it is simply a matter of time since it is the will of Allah.

The Sharia is the practical conclusion of political Islam. It is also a way for the non-Muslim to see how the Trilogy is the basis for not only a religion but also the most powerful political system in history. The Trilogy is both a political theory and a complete, detailed code of law that covers contract law, banking, family law, insurance, criminal law, and foreign policy.

The following are edited excerpts from a thirteen-hundred-year-old classic text, *The Reliance of the Traveller*.[1] Due to the fact that the Koran is considered to be the unchanging perfection and finality of Islam, it is still used today. Once you have read the Koran and the Hadith, you will recognize all of these laws. They are nothing more than a codified summary of both texts. The Sharia is the fruit of the doctrine of political Islam.

JIHAD

Jihad means to war against non-Muslims and is etymologically derived from the word *mujahada*, signifying warfare to establish the religion, which is the lesser jihad. As for the greater jihad, it is spiritual

---

1 Ahmad Ibn Naqib Al-Misri, *The Reliance of the Traveller, A Classic Manual of Islamic Sacred Law* (Amana Publications, 1994).

warfare against the lower self, which is why the Prophet said as he was returning from jihad, "We have returned from the lesser jihad to the greater jihad."

The scriptural basis for jihad, prior to scholarly consensus, is such Koranic verses as:

> (1) 2:216 *You are commanded to fight although you dislike it. You may hate something that is good for you, and love something that is bad for you. Allah knows and you do not.*
> (2) 4:89.... *But if they turn back, find them and kill them wherever they are.*
> (3)9:36... *Do not be unjust to yourselves regarding them, but fight the unbelievers as they fight you altogether.*

and such hadiths as the one related by Bukhari and Muslim that the Prophet said:

> "*I have been commanded to fight people until they testify that there is no god but Allah and that Muhammad is the Messenger of Allah, and perform the prayer, and pay zakat. If they say it, they have saved their blood and possessions from me, except for the rights of Islam over them. And their final reckoning is with Allah*";

and the hadith reported by Muslim,

> "*To go forth in the morning or evening to fight in the path of Allah is better than the whole world and everything in it.*"

Details concerning jihad are found in the accounts of the military expeditions of the Prophet, both his own and those on which he dispatched others. He personally led twenty-seven (others say twenty-nine); he fought in eight of them, killing only one person with his noble hand at the battle of Uhud. On the latter expeditions he sent others to fight, remaining at Medina; these were forty-seven in number. [This was over a period of nine years, or the average of one violent event every six weeks.]

It is unlawful for men or women to dye their hair black *except when the intention is jihad*. Plucking out gray hair is offensive. It is Sunna to dye the hair with yellow or red.

THE OBLIGATORY CHARACTER OF JIHAD

Jihad is a communal obligation. When enough people perform it successfully it is no longer obligatory upon others. The Prophet's saying,

"He who provides the equipment for a soldier in jihad has himself performed jihad,"

> 4:95 *Believers who stay at home in safety, other than those who are disabled, are not equal to those who fight with their wealth and their lives for Allah's cause [jihad]. Allah has ranked those who fight earnestly with their wealth and lives above those who stay at home. Allah has promised good things to all, but those who fight for Him will receive a far greater reward than those who have not.*

Jihad is personally obligatory upon all those present in the battle lines and to flee is a great error provided one is able to fight. If unable to fight, because of illness or the death of a soldiers mount, when not able to fight on foot, or because one no longer has a weapon, then the soldier may leave. He may also leave if the opposing non-Muslim army is more than twice the size of the Muslim force.

Jihad is also obligatory for everyone when the enemy has surrounded the Muslims, for non-Muslim forces entering Muslim lands is a weighty matter that cannot be ignored, but must be met with effort and struggle to repel them by every possible means.

WHO IS OBLIGED TO FIGHT IN JIHAD?

Every able-bodied man who has reached puberty and is sane is called upon.

THE OBJECTIVES OF JIHAD

The caliph makes war upon Jews, Christians, and Zoroastrians provided he has first invited them to enter Islam in faith and practice, and if they will not, then invite them to enter the social order of Islam by paying the non-Muslim poll tax (jizya).

> 9:29 *Make war on those who have received the Scriptures [Jews and Christians] but do not believe in Allah or in the Last Day. They do not forbid what Allah and His Messenger have forbidden. The Christians and Jews do not follow the religion of truth until they submit and pay the poll tax [jizya], and they are humiliated.*

FLEEING FROM COMBAT IN JIHAD

Allah Most High says,

8:16 *Anyone who turns his back on them, unless it is for a tactical advantage or to join another company, will incur Allah's wrath and Hell will be his home, truly a tortuous end*

THE RULES OF WARFARE

It is not permissible in jihad to kill women or children unless they are fighting against the Muslims. Nor is it permissible to kill animals, unless they are being ridden into battle against the Muslims, or if killing them will help defeat the enemy. It is permissible to kill old men and monks.

Whoever enters Islam before being captured may not be killed or his property confiscated, or his young children taken captive.

When a child or a woman is taken captive, they become slaves by the fact of capture, and the woman's previous marriage is immediately annulled.

It is permissible in jihad to cut down the enemies' trees and destroy their dwellings.

TRUCES

As for truces, the author does not mention them. In Sacred Law truce means a peace treaty with those hostile to Islam, involving a cessation of fighting for a specified period, whether for payment or something else.

There must be some interest served in making a truce other than mere preservation of the status quo. Allah Most High says,

47:35 *Therefore, do not be weak and offer the unbelievers peace when you have the upper hand for Allah is with you and will not begrudge you the reward of your deeds.*

Interests that justify making a truce are such things as Muslim weakness because of lack of numbers or materiel, or the hope an enemy will become Muslim, for the Prophet made a truce in the year Mecca was liberated with Safwan Ibn Umayya for four months in hope that he would become Muslim, and he entered Islam before the time was up. If the Muslims are weak, a truce may be made for ten years if necessary, for the Prophet made a truce with Quraysh for that long, as is related by Abu Dawud. It is not permissible to stipulate longer than that, save by means of new truces, each of which does not exceed ten years.

THE SPOILS OF BATTLE

A free male Muslim who has reached puberty and is sane is entitled to the spoils of battle when he has participated in a battle to the end of it.

After personal spoils of war, the collective spoils of the battle are divided into five parts. The first fifth is set aside, and the remaining four are distributed, one share to each infantryman and three shares to each cavalryman. From these latter four-fifths also is a token payment that is given at the leader's discretion to women, children, and non-Muslim participants on the Muslim side.

A combatant only takes possession of his share of the spoils at the official division.

As for personal spoils of war, anyone who, despite resistance, kills one of the enemy or effectively incapacitates him, risking his own life thereby, is entitled to whatever he can take from the enemy, meaning as much as he can take away with him in the battle, such as a mount, clothes, weaponry, money, or other.

NON-MUSLIM SUBJECTS OF THE ISLAMIC STATE, THE DHIMMI

A formal agreement of protection is made with citizens who are:
1. Jews
2. Christians
3. Zoroastrians
4. Samarians and Sabians, if their religions do not respectively contradict the fundamental bases of Judaism and Christianity.
5. Those who adhere to the religion of Abraham or one of the other prophets

Such an agreement may not be effected with those who are idol worshippers, or those who do not have a Sacred Book or something that could have been a Book.

Such an agreement is only valid when the subject peoples:
(a) follow the rules of Islam and those (*rules*) involving public behavior and dress, though in acts of worship and their private lives, the subject communities have their own laws, judges, and courts, enforcing the rules of their own religion among themselves
(b) and pay the non-Muslim poll tax (*jizya*)

THE NON-MUSLIM POLL TAX

Such non-Muslim subjects are obliged to comply with Islamic rules that pertain to the safety and indemnity of life, reputation, and property. In addition, they

1. Are penalized for committing adultery or theft, though not for drunkenness.

2. Are distinguished from Muslims in dress, wearing a wide cloth belt.

3. Are not greeted with "as-Salamu 'alaykum".

4. Must keep to the side of the street [always defer to a Muslim in the streets].

5. May not build higher than or as high as the Muslims' buildings, though if they acquire a tall house, it is not razed.

6. Are forbidden to openly display wine or pork, to ring church bells or display crosses, recite the Torah or Gospels aloud, or make public display of their funerals and feast days;

7. And are forbidden to build new churches.

They are forbidden to reside in the Hijaz, meaning the area and towns around Mecca, Medina, and Yamama, for more than three days (when the caliph allows them to enter there for something they need).

A non-Muslim may not enter the Meccan Sacred Precinct (Haram) under any circumstances, or enter any other mosque without permission, nor may Muslims enter churches without their permission.

It is obligatory for the caliph to protect those of them who are in Muslim lands just as he would Muslims, and to seek the release of those of them who are captured.

If non-Muslim subjects of the Islamic state refuse to conform to the rules of Islam, or to pay the non-Muslim poll tax, then their agreement with the state has been violated though if only one of them disobeys, it concerns him alone.

The agreement is also violated with respect to the offender alone if the state has stipulated that any of the following things break it, and one of the subjects does so anyway, though if the state has not stipulated that these break the agreement, then they do not; namely, if one of the subject people:

1. Commits adultery with a Muslim woman or marries her

2. Conceals spies of hostile forces

145

3. Leads a Muslim away from Islam

4. Kills a Muslim

5. Mentions something impermissible about Allah, the Prophet, or Islam

APOSTATES

Leaving Islam is the ugliest form of unbelief (*kafir*) and the worst.

When a person who has reached puberty and is sane voluntarily apostatizes from Islam, he deserves to be killed.

There is no indemnity for killing an apostate or any expiation, since it is killing someone who deserves to die.

If a spouse in a consummated marriage apostatizes from Islam, the couple are separated for a waiting period consisting of three intervals between menstruations. If the spouse returns to Islam before the waiting period ends, the marriage is not annulled but is considered to have continued the whole time.

THE PENALTY FOR FORNICATION OR SODOMY

The legal penalty is obligatorily imposed upon anyone who fornicates or commits sodomy when they have reached puberty, are sane, and commit the act voluntarily, no matter whether the person is a Muslim, non-Muslim subject of the Islamic state, or someone who has left Islam.

An offender is not scourged in intense heat or bitter cold, or when he is ill and recovery is expected (until he recovers), or in a mosque, or when the offender is a woman who is pregnant, until she gives birth and has recovered from childbed pains. The whip used should be neither new nor old and worn-out, but something in between. The offender is not stretched out when scourged, or bound as his hands are left loose to fend off blows, or undressed, and the scourger does not lay the stripes on hard (by raising his arm, such that he draws blood). The scourger distributes the blows over various parts of the body, avoiding the vital points and the face. A man is scourged standing; a woman, sitting and covered. If the offender is emaciated, or sick from an illness not expected to improve, then he or she is scourged with a single date palm frond upon which there are a hundred stripes, or fifty. If a hundred, such an offender is struck once with it, and if fifty, then twice, or with the edge of a garment.

If the penalty is stoning, the offender is stoned even in severe heat or cold, and even if he has an illness from which he is expected to recover. A pregnant woman is not stoned until she gives birth and the child can suffice with the milk of another.

SODOMY AND LESBIANISM

In more than one place in the Holy Koran, Allah recounts to us the story of Lot's people, and how He destroyed them for their wicked practice. There is consensus among both Muslims and the followers of all other religions that the sin of sodomy is an enormity. It is even more vile and uglier than adultery.

Allah Most High says:

> 26:165 *What? Of all the creatures of the world, will you have sexual relations with men? Will you ignore your wives whom Allah has created for you? You people exceed all limits!"*

The Prophet said:

1. Kill the one who sodomizes and the one who lets it be done to him.

2. May Allah curse him who does what Lot's people did.

3. Lesbianism by women is adultery between them.

MASCULINE WOMEN AND EFFEMINATE MEN

The Prophet said:

1) Men are already destroyed when they obey women.

2) The Prophet cursed effeminate men and masculine women.

3) The Prophet cursed men who wear women's clothing and women who wear men's.

THE WIFE'S MARITAL OBLIGATIONS

> 4:34 *Allah has made men superior to women because men spend their wealth to support them. Therefore, virtuous women are obedient, and they are to guard their unseen parts as Allah has guarded them. As for women whom you fear will rebel, admonish them first, and then send them to a separate bed, and then beat them. But if they are disobedient after that, then do nothing further; surely Allah is exalted and great!*

> 2:223 *Your women are your plowed fields: go into your fields when you like, but do some good deed beforehand and fear Allah. Keep in mind that you will meet Him. Give good news to the believers.*

It is obligatory for a woman to let her husband have sex with her immediately when he asks her; at home; and she can physically endure it.

(d) Another condition that should be added is that her marriage payment has been received.

As for when sex with her is not possible, such that having it would entail manifest harm to her, then she is not obliged to comply.

THE HUSBAND'S RIGHTS

A husband possesses full right to enjoy his wife's person from the top of her head to the bottoms of her feet—though anal intercourse is absolutely unlawful—in what does not physically harm her.

He is entitled to take her with him when he travels.

PERMITTING ONE'S WIFE TO LEAVE THE HOUSE

A husband may permit his wife to leave the house for a lesson in Sacred Law, for invocation of Allah, to see her female friends, or to go to any place in the town. A woman may not leave the city without her husband or a member of her unmarriageable kin accompanying her unless the journey is obligatory, like the hajj. It is unlawful for her to travel otherwise, and unlawful for her husband to allow her to travel.

The husband may forbid his wife to leave the home because of the hadith related by Bukhari that the Prophet said,

"It is not permissible for a woman who believes in Allah and the Last Day to allow someone into her husband's house if he is opposed, or to go out if he is averse".

DEALING WITH A REBELLIOUS WIFE

When a husband notices signs of rebelliousness in his wife whether in words as when she answers him coldly when she used to do so politely; or he asks her to come to bed and she refuses, contrary to her usual habit; or whether in acts, as when he finds her averse to him when she was previously kind and cheerful, he warns her in words without keeping from her or hitting her, for it may be that she has an excuse.

The warning could be to tell her, "Fear Allah concerning the rights you owe to me,"

Or it could be to explain that rebelliousness nullifies his obligation to support her and give her a turn amongst other wives, or it could be to inform her, "Your obeying me is religiously obligatory."

If she commits rebelliousness, he keeps from sleeping (having sex) with her without words and may hit her but not in a way that injures her, meaning he may not bruise her, break bones, wound her, or cause blood to flow. It is unlawful to strike another's face. He may hit her whether she is rebellious only once or whether more than once, though a weaker opinion holds that he may not hit her unless there is repeated rebelliousness.

To clarify this paragraph, we mention the following rulings:

1. Both man and wife are obliged to treat each other kindly and graciously.

2. It is not lawful for a wife to leave the house except by the permission of her husband, though she may do so without permission when there is a pressing necessity. Nor may a wife permit anyone to enter her husband's home unless he agrees, even their unmarriageable kin. Nor may she be alone with a non-family member male, under any circumstances.

3. It is obligatory for a wife to obey her husband as is customary in allowing him full lawful sexual enjoyment of her person. It is obligatory for the husband to enable her to remain chaste and free of want for sex if he is able.

4. If the wife does not fulfill one of the above mentioned obligations, she is termed "rebellious", and the husband takes the following steps to correct matters:

(a) admonition and advice, by explaining the unlawfulness of rebellion, its harmful effect on married life, and by listening to her viewpoint on the matter

(b) if admonition is ineffectual, he keeps from her by not sleeping in bed with her, by which both learn the degree to which they need each other

(c) if keeping from her is ineffectual, *it is permissible for him to hit her* if he believes that hitting her will bring her back to the right path, though if he does not think so, it is not permissible. *His hitting her may not be in a way that injures her*, and is his last recourse to save the family

THE CONDITIONS THAT ENTITLE A WIFE TO SUPPORT

The husband is only obliged to support his wife when she gives herself to him or offers to, meaning she allows him full enjoyment of her person and does not refuse him sex at any time of the night or day.

She is not entitled to support from her husband when the following occurs:

1. She is rebellious (meaning when she does not obey him) even if for a moment.

2. She travels without his permission, or with his permission but for one of her own needs.

INJURIES

There is no indemnity obligatory for killing a non-Muslim at war with Muslims, someone who has left Islam, someone sentenced to death by stoning for adultery (by virtue of having been convicted in court), or those it is obligatory to kill by military action.

> 4:92 *A believer should never kill a Muslim unless an accident occurs. Whoever kills a fellow Muslim by accident must free one of his believing slaves and pay blood-money to the victim's family unless they give it to charity. If the victim was a believer from a people at war with you, then freeing a believing slave is enough. But if the victim was from a people with whom you have an alliance, then his family should be paid blood-money and a believing slave must be set free. For those who cannot afford to do this, they must fast for two months straight. This is the penance commanded by Allah. Allah is all-knowing and wise!*
>
> 4:93 *For those who intentionally kill another Muslim, Hell will be their punishment, where they will live forever. The wrath of Allah will be upon*

EPILOGUE

CHAPTER 24

POLITICS

The doctrine of the Trilogy culminates in the dominance of political Islam. The Trilogy teaches that Islam is the perfect political system and is destined to rule the entire world. The governments and constitutions of the world must all submit to political Islam. If the political systems of the unbelievers do not submit, then force, jihad, may be used. All jihad is defensive, since refusing to submit to Islam is an offense against Allah. All Muslims must support the political action of jihad. This may take several forms—fighting, proselytizing or contributing money.

The basis of the Islamic dualistic legal code, the Sharia, is found in the Trilogy. The Sharia treats non-Muslims, including Jews and Christians, as inferior to believers. This legal inferiority is sacred, eternal and universal.

Islamic Hell is primarily political. Hell is mentioned 146 times in the Koran. Only 9 references are for moral failings—greed, lack of charity, love of worldly success. The other 137 references to Hell involve eternal torture for disagreeing with Mohammed. Thus 94 percent of the references to Hell are as a political prison for dissenters.

THE KORAN AND PHILOSOPHY

The Trilogy lays out a complete philosophic system including politics and ethics. Its metaphysics claim that the only reality is Allah and humanity is to worship Him. Human life has been pre-determined by Allah. The highest form of living is to die for Allah in jihad. Death, Paradise, and Hell are the values of Islam. The proper relationship between Allah and humanity is master/slave (Muslims are the slaves of Allah) and fear (there are over 300 references to the fear of Allah, the Merciful).

The epistemology (what is knowledge and how knowledge is acquired) of the Trilogy and Islam is revelation. But since Mohammed is the final prophet, the door to further knowledge is closed.

DUALITY

The constant theme of Islam's perfect, eternal, and universal Trilogy is the division between those who believe Mohammed, and those who don't. This sacred division is dualism; nonbelievers are not fully human and fall under a separate moral code. The dualistic separation is in politics, culture and religion. This duality is carried further by two different approaches to the unbeliever in the Koran of Mecca and the Koran of Medina.

Some verses of the Koran contradict each other, but the text states a principle for resolving the contradictions. The later verse nullifies the earlier verse. However, since the entire Koran comes from Allah, then all verses are true, and no verse is actually false. The later, contradictory verse is merely stronger than the earlier, weaker verse. In practice, both sides of a contradiction can be true—logical duality.

LOGIC

The Trilogy advances a logical system. Truth is determined by revelation. No fact or argument may refute the Trilogy. Logical persuasion is based upon repetition and continued assertion. Another part of the persuasion is personal attacks against those who resist Islam. The Trilogy advances its argument through threats against specific people and groups. If persuasion fails, then force may be used to settle the logical or political argument.

Another aspect of Koranic logic is the use of name-calling and personal insults to advance the truth. The Koran, with its poetical language and repeated threats and physical violence, bases its logic on emotions. Although its intellectual truth can be contradictory, the contradictions do not need to be resolved. Understanding apparent contradictions is a key to understanding Islamic logic. In unitary logic, a contradiction shows the theory or argument is false. But in the Koran, a contradiction does not prove an argument to be false. What appears to be logical contradictions are statements of duality that offer two true choices, depending upon the circumstances. This is a dualistic logic.

How do we know that the Koran is true? Because it contains the words of Allah. How do we know that these are the words of Allah? Mohammed said they were Allah's words. How do we know that Mohammed is Allah's messenger? Mohammed reported that Allah said that Mohammed is His messenger.

ETHICS

The ethical system of the Trilogy is also dualistic. How a person is treated depends upon his being a believer or an unbeliever. There is one set of ethics for the believer and another set of ethics for the unbeliever. Deceit, violence and force are acceptable against the unbelievers who resist the logic of the Koran. Believers are to be treated as brothers and sisters. Good is whatever advances Islam. Evil is whatever resists Islam.

THE REFORM OF ISLAM

When people first learn about the actual doctrine contained in the Trilogy, a frequent response is that Islam needs a reformation like Christianity experienced.

First, what does it matter if the religion reforms or not? It is the politics that produce fear.

The doctrine of Islam is proclaimed to be eternal, universal and perfect. Eternal means unchanging and final. Mohammed is the final and last prophet of Allah. "Universal" means that it applies to all of the world and "perfect" means that the doctrine needs no change.

A problem with reformation is the amount of political doctrine. About two thirds of the Koran of Mecca deals with condemning unbelievers to Hell for merely disagreeing with Mohammed. Over half of the Koran of Medina deals with hypocrites and jihad against unbelievers. Nearly 75 percent of the Sira deals with jihad. About 20 percent of the Hadith by Bukhari is about jihad. The majority of the doctrine is political and it is all violent. Removing this doctrine would destroy political Islam.

A common justification for Islamic reform is that the horrible acts are medieval, tribal customs and in modern times we don't do that sort of thing.

But for a Muslim, the Koran is perfect and eternal. And the Koran relentlessly advances the idea that the *Sunna* (the words and deeds of Mohammed) is the ideal mode of Islamic behavior. Both the Koran and the Hadith are very clear that the medieval, tribal actions are the ideal for humanity and far from being put in the dust bin of history, they are the perfect guidance for today.

The dilemma of removing medieval-tribalism is that much of the Trilogy consists of medieval-tribalism. So if you reform political Islam by taking out the old tribal doctrine, where do you stop? What is the guidance for which old, tribal acts of Mohammed are not applicable for today?

You can't take it all out. Without medieval-tribalism there is basically no Islam.

And what body of Islam has the authority to reform it? There is no such authority. Some group of Muslims might decide to drop all of the violent and oppressive political doctrine, but what authority would they have to tell any other Muslim to follow them? Then there is the question of why would any Muslim want reform? Demographic jihad (immigration) will cause Europe to be Islamic in less than a century. Based upon immigration and birth rates, France will be an Islamic nation in 2020 AD and all of Europe will become Eurabia by the end of the 21st century. Islam is winning. Why reform a winner?

Another difficulty with reformation is the incredible amount of detail regarding politics. Islam is detailed down to the smallest action of life and living, and there is a vast quantity of detail that allows very little room for interpretation or change.

Then there is the matter of Islam's dualistic ethics. How do you reform the ethical system that is at the core of Islam?

The doctrine of Islam can no more be reformed than a circle can be reformed by putting corners on it. It is logically impossible. Islamic doctrine is defined as unchanging and beyond reform. The Koran is perfect and eternal. Mohammed is the final prophet and the ideal model for all humanity for all times. The reformation of the doctrine of Islam is logically impossible.

MOHAMMED AND SLAVERY

The term *slave* is a positive one in Islam. Mohammed referred to himself and Muslims as the slaves of Allah. Mohammed's second convert was a slave.

Mohammed himself was involved in every single aspect of slavery. He had non-believing men killed so their women and children could be made slaves[1]. He gave slaves away for gifts[2]. He owned many slaves, some of them black[3]. He passed around slaves for the purpose of sex to his companions, men who were his chief lieutenants[4]. He stood by while others beat slaves[5].

1. A. Guillaume, *The Life of Muhammad* (London: Oxford University Press, 1982), 466.
2. Ibid., p. 499.
3. Ibid., p. 516.
4. Ibid., p. 593.
5. Ibid., p. 295.

He shared the pleasure of forced sex with women slaves after conquest[6]. He captured slaves and wholesaled them to raise money for jihad[7]. One of his favorite sexual partners was a slave, who bore him a son[8]. He got slaves as gifts from other rulers[9]. The very pulpit he preached from was made by a slave[10]. He ate food prepared by slaves[11]. He was treated medically by a slave[12]. He had a slave tailor[13]. He declared that a slave who ran away from his master would not have his prayers answered[14]. And he approved an owner's having sex with his slaves[15].

RELIGION

Some English translations of the Koran use the word God instead of Allah. In an English speaking culture the word God is synonymous with the One-God, Jehovah/Yahweh, of the Jews and Christians. However, the meaning of both Allah and Jehovah/Yahweh is based upon their textual attributes. Allah is defined by the Koran. Jehovah/Yahweh is defined by the Old Testament. On a textual basis Jews, Muslims, and Christians do not worship the same God. As an example, red and blue are both colors, but red is not blue. Likewise, Allah and Jehovah/Yahweh are both a One-God, but they are not the same One-God. Allah is not Jehovah/Yahweh[16]. Hence, Allah is the only acceptable term for the One-God of the Koran.

6. Ibid., p. 496.
7. Ibid., p. 466.
8. William Muir, *The Life of Mohammed* (AMS Press, 1975), 425.
9. Ibid., p. 425.
10. Bukhari, Hadith, Volume 1, Book 8, Number 440.
11. Ibid., Volume 3, Book 34, Number 295.
12. Ibid., Volume 3, Book 36, Number 481.
13. Ibid., Volume 7, Book 65, Number 344.
14. Muslim, Hadith, Book 001, Number 0131.
15. Ibid., Book 008, Number 3383.
16. Arab Christians also use the word Allah. The word allah is derived from *ilah*, deity or god, and *al*, meaning the. So Allah means The-God. But the meaning of the name Allah of Arab Christians is taken from the Christian scriptures. The meaning of the name Allah of Islam comes from the Koran. The Allah of Arab Christians is not the Allah of Islam. But for Arab Christians Allah is the same as Jehovah.

NAMING

All of the names and terms used by Islam come from the Trilogy. But unbelievers don't use these terms or names.

The jihad of Umar burst out of Arabia and crushed the Christian world of Syria, Egypt, and the rest of the Middle East. The Christians recorded it as an Arabic war. When Islam invaded Europe, Europeans called it a Turkish invasion. The jihad against Christian Spain was an invasion by the Moors. The Muslims called these events jihad.

In the early nineteenth century America sent the Navy and Marines to war against the Barbary pirates on the Berber coast in north Africa. For centuries the Islamic Barbary pirates had raided Europe and taken nearly a million white slaves, and their shipping raids in the Mediterranean had taken a great toll. But the Muslims never called their naval raiders "Barbary pirates." They called them *ghazis,* sacred raiders. A raid led by Mohammed against the unbelievers' caravans was called a *ghazwah.* The Muslims were clear that naval raids by the "Barbary pirates" were actually jihad by the army of Mohammed. Naming them "pirates" showed that the unbelievers had no idea about the doctrine and history of Islam.

Look at the news today. The media report an *intifada,* uprising, by the Palestinians against the Israelis. But the terms *intifada, Palestinian,* and *Israeli* are misnomers. The real terms are *jihad, Muslim* and *infidel,* if we follow the Koran. The doctrine of political Islam clearly states that jihad is to be waged by all Muslims against all Jews and other "unbelievers." Today is no different from 1400 years ago in Islam.

The events of 9/11 are recorded in the West as an attack by terrorists. Mohammed Atta, the leader of the 9/11 attackers, was a pious Muslim. He left a letter clearly stating his intentions: 9/11 was pure jihad. An attack is a single event, but jihad is a 1400-year continuous process. Therefore, a terrorist attack is not the same as jihad. *Terrorism* does not have the same meaning as *jihad.*

When immigrant violence erupted in France in 2005, unbelievers called them the "Paris riots." Muslims called the burnings and theft the "Great Ramadan Offensive," which connects them to Mohammed's first jihad in the sacred month of Ramadan. The name "Paris riots" evokes a much different set of thoughts, insights, and points of view from the "Great Ramadan Offensive."

The naming of these events by unbelievers does not convey the right meaning. Muslims' names for themselves and their actions connect events and people with Islamic history and doctrine and show a continuing process. Non-Muslim names are temporary, do not connect events, and show no historic process.

What do the terms "moderate Muslim" and "extremist Muslim" actually mean? Only Islam can define what a Muslim is. According to the Trilogy, a Muslim is anyone who follows the pattern (Sunna) of Mohammed. What unbelievers call a moderate, *i.e.* peaceful, Muslim is actually a Muslim behaving as Mohammed did when he lived in Mecca. And an extremist Muslim is really a Medinan Muslim, one following the words and actions of the Prophet when he lived in Medina. Unbelievers call Osama Bin Laden an extremist Muslim, but his actions are carefully based upon those of Mohammed in Medina. Bin Laden, like all jihadists, is a devout Muslim following the Koran of Medina. As far as the Koran is concerned, an extremist Muslim is one who leaves the religion, an apostate.

The only correct terms are those of Islam. The names applied to these events by unbelievers are wrong because those names are a projection of Western culture. Correct naming leads to correct thinking.

TRANSLATING THE KORAN

Islam frequently claims that the Koran cannot be translated. Most of the Koran is written in a poetic style that is similar to the ancient classical texts such as the Greek *Odyssey*. The *Odyssey* is an epic story that is written in poetry, which makes it possible to memorize it. The Koran is also written, for the most part, in a poetic form that is easy to memorize.

Take an English proverb: "Birds of a feather, flock together." We have the information that a flock of birds only contains one type of bird, but it is written in poetic form. Can "Birds of a feather, flock together" be translated into Arabic? No. But the meaning of "a flock of birds contains only one type of bird," can be easily translated into Arabic.

The poetry of the Koran does not translate, but the meaning of the Koran can be translated. Read many different translations of the Koran and you will find the meaning is consistent across the translations.

So, can the Koran be translated? No. Can the meaning be translated into any other language? Yes. If the meaning of a particular part of the Koran cannot be translated, then that implies that the concept is not applicable to that language. Or said another way, that part of the Koran would not be universal. But the Koran is very insistent upon the fact that it is universal. So by definition of universal, it follows that the universal meaning can be translated into all languages.

A COMMON MISCONCEPTION

Most nonbelievers think that the Koran is the basis of Islam, but Islam is founded equally upon the words of Allah (the Koran) and the Sunna (the words and actions of Mohammed found in the Sira and the Hadith). The words of Allah represent only about 17 percent of the total doctrinal texts. The words and actions of Mohammed comprise 83 percent of the doctrine of Islam.

THE TEARS OF JIHAD

These figures are a rough estimate of the death of non-Muslims by the political act of jihad.

AFRICA

Thomas Sowell estimates that eleven million slaves were shipped across the Atlantic and fourteen million were sent to the Islamic nations of North Africa and the Middle East[1]. For every slave captured many others died. Estimates of this collateral damage vary. The renowned missionary David Livingstone estimated that for every slave who reached the plantation five others died by being killed in the raid or died on the forced march from illness and privation.[2] Those who were left behind were the very young, the weak, the sick and the old. These soon died since their main providers had been killed or enslaved. So, for twenty-five million slaves delivered to the market, we have the death of about 120 million people. Muslims ran the wholesale slave trade in Africa.

120 million Africans

CHRISTIANS

The number of Christians martyred by Islam is nine million.[3] A rough estimate by Raphael Moore in *History of Asia Minor* is that another fifty million died in wars by jihad. So to account for the one million African Christians killed in the 20th century we have:##

60 million Christians

---

1. Thomas Sowell, *Race and Culture*, BasicBooks, 1994, p. 188.
2. Woman's Presbyterian Board of Missions, *David Livingstone,* p. 62, 1888.
3. David B. Barrett, Todd M. Johnson, *World Christian Trends AD 30-AD 2200*, William Carey Library, 2001, p. 230, table 4-10.

HINDUS

Koenard Elst in *Negationism in India*[1] gives an estimate of eighty million Hindus killed in the total jihad against India. The country of India today is only half the size of ancient India, due to jihad. The mountains near India are called the Hindu Kush, meaning the "funeral pyre of the Hindus".

80 million Hindus

BUDDHISTS

Buddhists do not keep up with the history of war. Keep in mind that in jihad only Christians and Jews were allowed to survive as dhimmis (servants to Islam); everyone else had to convert or die. Jihad killed the Buddhists in Turkey, Afghanistan, along the Silk Route, and in India. The total is roughly ten million.[2]

10 million Buddhists

JEWS

Oddly enough there were not enough Jews killed in jihad to significantly affect the totals of the Great Annihilation. The jihad in Arabia was 100 percent effective but the numbers were in the thousands, not millions. After that the Jews submitted and became the dhimmis (servants and second class citizens) of Islam and did not have geographic political power.

TOTAL

This gives a rough estimate of **270 million** killed by jihad.

---

1. Koenard Elst, *Negationism in India*, Voice of India, New Delhi, 2002, pg. 34.
2. David B. Barrett, Todd M. Johnson, *World Christian Trends AD 30-AD 2200*, William Carey Library, 2001, p. 230, table 4-1.

BIBLIOGRAPHY

Watt, W. Montgomery and Bell, Richard. *Introduction to the Quran.* Edinburgh: Edinburgh University Press, 1970.

Robinson, Neal. *Discovering the Koran.* London: SCM Press, 1996.

Arberry, A. J. *The Koran Interpreted,* NY: Touchstone, 1996.

Pickthall, Mohammed M. *The Meaning of the Glorious Koran.* Kuwait: Dar al-Islamiyya.

Warraq, Ibn. *What the Koran Really Says.* Amherst, NY: Prometheus Books, 2002.

Dawood, N. J. *The Koran,* London: Penguin Books, 1999.

Rodwell, J. M. *The Koran,* North Clarendon, VT: Tuttle Publishing, 1994.

Ali, Maulana Muhammad. *Holy Koran.* Columbus, Ohio: Ahmadiyyah Anjuman Ishaat Islam 1998.

Watt, W. Montgomery and M.V. McDonald. *The History of al-Tabari, vol. VI, Muhammad at Mecca.* New York: The State University of New York Press, 1987.

McDonald, M.V. and W. Montgomery Watt. *The History of al-Tabari, vol. VII, The Foundation of the Community.* New York: The State University of New York Press, 1987.

Michael Fishbone, *The History of al-Tabari VIII The Victory of Islam.* New York: The State University of New York Press, 1987.

Poonawala, Ismail K. *The History of al-Tabari, vol. IX, The Last Years of the Prophet.* New York: The State University of New York Press, 1987.

Muir, Sir William. *Life of Mohammed.* New York: AMS Press, 1975.

Guillaume, A. *The Life of Muhammad,* (Ishaq's—*Sirat Rasul Allah*). Karachi: Oxford University Press, 1967.

The Hadith of Abu Al-Bukhari, *Sahih Bukhari,* and the Hadith of Abu Muslim, *Sahih Muslim,* are best found on the internet. The University of Southern California is one of the best sites.

Printed in the United States
66896LVS00005B/118-138

9 780978 552831